RUDOLF STEINER (1861–1925) called his spiritual philosophy 'anthroposophy', meaning 'wisdom of the human being'. As a highly developed seer, he based his work on direct knowledge and perception of spiritual dimensions. He initiated a modern and universal 'science of spirit', accessible to anyone willing to exercise clear and unprejudiced thinking.

From his spiritual investigations Steiner provided suggestions for the renewal of many activities, including education (both general and special), agriculture, medicine, economics, architecture, science, philosophy, religion and the arts. Today there are thousands of schools, clinics, farms and other organizations involved in practical work based on his principles. His many published works feature his research into the spiritual nature of the human being, the evolution of the world and humanity, and methods of personal development. Steiner wrote some 30 books and delivered over 6000 lectures across Europe. In 1924 he founded the General Anthroposophical Society, which today has branches throughout the world.

In the deep ground of our soul
lives, sure to triumph, spirit sun;
true powers of the feeling mind
can sense this in the inward life
of winter; and heart's springing hope
sees sun spirit's victory shine
in the blessed light of Christmas: as
an image of the highest life
in deep winter's darkest night.

CHRISTMAS

Festivals

Also available:

(Festivals)
Easter
Michaelmas
St John's
Whitsun

(Practical Applications)
Agriculture
Architecture
Art
Education
Eurythmy
Medicine
Religion
Science
Social and Political Science

(Esoteric)
Alchemy
Atlantis
Christian Rozenkreutz
The Druids
The Goddess
The Holy Grail

RUDOLF STEINER

CHRISTMAS
An Introductory Reader

*Compiled with an introduction,
commentary and notes by
Matthew Barton*

Sophia Books

Sophia Books
An imprint of Rudolf Steiner Press
Hillside House, The Square
Forest Row, RH18 5ES

www.rudolfsteinerpress.com

Published by Rudolf Steiner Press 2007

For earlier English publications of individual selections please
see pp. 155–6

The material by Rudolf Steiner was originally published in
German in various volumes of the 'GA' (*Rudolf Steiner
Gesamtausgabe* or Collected Works) by Rudolf Steiner Verlag,
Dornach. This authorized volume is published by permission of
the Rudolf Steiner Nachlassverwaltung, Dornach (for further
information see pp. 159–60)

All translations revised by Matthew Barton

*Matthew Barton would like to thank Margaret Jonas, librarian at Rudolf
Steiner House, for her invaluable help in locating volumes used in
compiling this book.*

A catalogue record for this book is available from the British
Library

ISBN 978 185584 189 5

Cover by Andrew Morgan
Typeset by DP Photosetting, Neath, West Glamorgan
Printed by Cromwell Press Ltd., Trowbridge, Wiltshire

Contents

Introduction

Nearly 21 years ago my daughter was born on a cold January night. I witnessed the birth, and held my child—like holding a miracle, a new flame; then, in the small hours I left her and my wife in the hospital and phoned for a taxi. Everything seemed transformed, renewed, incandescent, even at that drab time long before dawn. The taxi arrived and I got in—and found myself face to face with, possibly, the ugliest, oddest man I've ever seen. It was not just his physical features that were alarming, but his whole demeanour. On another occasion I might have chosen to walk instead, but the sense of grace wrapping and flooding me allowed me to see this stranger in a different guise. I thought: 'You too were once newborn ...' I remember no particular words passing between us, only that I was lifted beyond fear or suspicion to a quite unsullied place in myself that could recognize the innocence, however deeply hidden, in another.

It is, perhaps, something of this sense that Steiner conjures in many of these lectures: the love, and the nature of the love, that can transport us in the presence of a newborn, innocent soul, and that

connects us with our own primal innocence—
inevitably lost in the forests of earthly experience.

Jungle might be a better word. Or wasteland. It is
very difficult to know how to celebrate Christmas
today—to reach back to that original innocence we
descend from on the one hand, and on the other to
reach forward to, and be informed by, a future
Christmas of heartfelt accord amongst humanity
that we are still so far from attaining. Between past
and future stands the present, a continual gift, if we
fully understand it, both of our long-gone origin
and far-off destination. Christmas, the most celebrated of Christian festivals, has for that very
reason succumbed most to the nature of modern
consciousness. Celebration of a purely physical
birth, of a very elevated but nevertheless merely
human and physical being, finds its counterpart in
a season of merely material gifts, and either sentimental or ironic expressions of good will.

Steiner has no objection at all to the warm con-
viviality among human beings which still survives
at this season despite the best efforts of commerce
to exploit it for profitable ends. But he says we need
something more, since the old sense of community
has lost its sustaining power and cannot effectively
be resuscitated by narrowing the world—as we all
do—to close(d) concerns of immediate family and
friends. Christmas so easily becomes a festival of

enhanced and divisive egotism, not of true remembrance and anticipation of our once and future united humanity, beyond all ties of blood. A parent's deep love for a child is absolutely authentic, but nevertheless it needs to broaden into an embrace of the whole world.

It is Steiner's concern in these extracts to forge a new Christmas—which means a new conscious-ness—seeking, on the one hand, for the deeper significance of the traditional symbols of child, tree, angel, shepherds and kings that nowadays are more or less drowned out by the jingle bells of cash tills, and on the other delving further and futurewards in our evolving understanding of the nature of Christ. There is no mention of Advent in these extracts, yet the whole evolution of humanity can be seen as a gradual approach to what approaches us in the figure of Christ. This may be something like the process described by Michelangelo of carving down into the form already present, concealed in the stone, which emerges towards us as we reach towards it with ever subtler, finer craft until the artist—in this case all humanity—meets its destined union with its deepest intention.

One of Steiner's essential insights, which may be very difficult for modern folk to countenance, is that Jesus and Christ are not one and the same, but that the former provided a vessel for a wholly non-material force and love to infuse, penetrate and renew the material earth. Materialists will long since have parted company with me, but this for Steiner is the core of the matter and in making it so he asks us to change our mind, heart and actions, opening ourselves to the future which can only approach us as we work transformatively on ourselves — and so on everybody else.

The double meaning of that little word 'present' can sum it all up. Perhaps the greatest gift an adult can offer a child is to be fully present with him. This sounds simple but is, of course, extremely difficult. We absent ourselves so easily, escaping into predetermined modes of behaviour, or taking flight into self-absorption of one kind or another. Presence of mind, if only for brief moments, enables us to be fully, lovingly available. Children know when we're wholly there for them — even if subtly and undemonstratively — and are past masters at urging this from us, often almost against our will. This meaning of present leads seamlessly into the other. When we really take care in choosing or making a gift for someone, something of the non-material quality of love we invest in the gift will communicate itself to the person receiving it. There is matter, certainly, in the gift's physical existence, but it is pervaded by our presence of mind — a spiritual gift. This image of spirit and matter joining hands, as it were, to create the present in both senses, is a tiny reflection of the great deed by the being called Christ who embraces, renews and transfigures the darkness and dead weight of earth, and seeds it with inner light. Throughout these lectures Steiner refers to this deed as the 'Mystery of Golgotha', but makes clear that he includes Christmas in this (see section 18, paragraph 3).

The passages and extracts collected here are just that—longer or shorter extracts from the larger context of whole lectures. Steiner developed his lectures into an art form in the best sense, and the reader is referred to the original, complete lectures for the 'total experience' and context from which these passages are drawn.

Matthew Barton

CHRISTMAS IN A GRIEVOUS AGE

1. Can We Celebrate Christmas?

Extract from a lecture given in Stuttgart on
25 December 1919

*No, says Steiner, in answer to this question, unless we
make Christmas an all-inclusive festival of humanity, and
do not shy away from facing the real state of the world
and its suffering.*

In recent years, whenever I spoke about any of the
great festivals of the year, Christmas, Easter or
Whitsun, I felt bound to say that we have no right
on such occasions to commemorate these festivals
in the old, accustomed manner. We have no right to
forget the widespread suffering, the widespread
sorrow of our times, and to recall only the greatest,
most incisive event in earthly evolution. Standing
as we do on the foundations of a spiritual view of
the world, it is our duty to allow all symptoms of
decline in human civilization today to permeate our
thoughts and penetrate right through to the
Christmas tree. It is our particular duty to receive
the birth of Christ Jesus into our hearts, into our

souls, in such a way that we do not close our eyes to
the fearful deterioration that has overtaken the so-
called civilized world.

On this day particularly we need to ask whether
the whole idea of Christmas has also succumbed to
the forces of general decline. When Christmas is
spoken of today do we still sense what we should
sense when we raise our thoughts and feelings to
contemplate the festival of Christ? Are people in
general conscious of the true meaning of what
entered human evolution at the Mystery of
Golgotha?[1]

We light up our Christmas tree, we repeat the
customary words and phrases associated with the
Christmas festival, but all too often we avoid
opening our eyes fully, we avoid awakening fully to
the need to acknowledge that here too there is
decline. We avoid asking: 'Where are you, O Christ
power, to actively bring about a new ascent?' It
must be clear to you from the lectures given in our
circles over many years that only the power of
Christ is capable of permeating declining civilization with an impulse that can regenerate it anew ...

It hardly means anything to thousands, to millions of people of the present day when they speak
of the festival of Christmas; for they know nothing
of the reality of Christ in the sense that is so
necessary for our time. We must examine these

things if we wish to gain a deeper understanding of the causes of degeneration and decline apparent in contemporary events, and in human life connected with these events.

Only through striving for spiritual truth is the real Christ to be sought and found; otherwise it would be better to extinguish the lights of Christmas, to destroy all Christmas trees, and to acknowledge the truth fully at least, that we want nothing that will recall what Christ Jesus brought to human evolution.

2. Christ Beyond Strife

Excerpt from a lecture given in Berlin on
19 December 1915

*There is irony, of course, in the fact that opposing sides in
a vicious conflict both call on the same God. Steiner takes
this fact, however, as the token of a force in the world –
Christ – that can ultimately heal all division and strife. It
was only one year before the date of this lecture, after all,
that German and English soldiers climbed out of their
trenches along much of the 500-mile western front on
Christmas day, 1914, to celebrate an unauthorized
Christmas truce. Hesitantly at first, men on both sides
stumbled into No Man's Land, shook hands, sang carols,
lit each other's cigarettes, swapped tunic buttons and
addresses and, most famously, played football, kicking
around empty bully-beef cans and using their caps or
steel helmets as goalposts.*

Nations confront one another full of animosity.
Blood, so much blood, saturates our earth. We have
witnessed and must feel countless deaths around us
now. Infinite suffering is interwoven with our inner

atmosphere of feeling. Hate and antipathy race through mental space and can easily show how far human beings in our time still are from that love spoken about by the One whose birth is celebrated at Christmas. One thought, however, predominates. We think how enemy opposes enemy, opponent stands against opponent, how human beings can bring death to each other, and how they can then pass through the same threshold of death with the thought of the divine light-bearer, Christ Jesus. We think of how, all over the earth, where there is war and pain and discord, those who are otherwise in such discord can be united. Within their deepest hearts they carry their connection with him who entered the world on the day we celebrate Christmas.

Let us recall that through all the animosity, antipathy, hatred, a feeling can impress itself into all human souls everywhere in these times, can impress itself in the midst of blood and hate: the thought of their innermost connection with the One who united hearts through something higher than what divides human beings on earth. And so the thought of Christ Jesus who reconciles human beings no matter what their discord might be, who creates harmony between them no matter what occurs in the world, is one of infinite greatness, infinite depth of feeling.

If we take hold of this thought, try to grasp it more intensely—especially in our time—we can have an intimation of how strongly this thought is connected with what must become great and powerful within human evolution. If this were to happen, much that still has to be fought for in such a bloodthirsty way nowadays could be achieved in another way by human hearts and souls.

3. Empty Phrase or Inner Peace?

Excerpt from a lecture given in Dornach on
24 December 1920

*Christmas is meaningless, says Steiner, unless it enlarges
our small concerns into ever wider, all-embracing circles,
and gives us an impetus to develop real community.*

For many modern people Christmas is nothing but
an occasion for giving and receiving presents,
something they celebrate each year through habit.
The Christmas festival has become an empty
phrase, like so many other things in modern life ...
This must change in future, so that instead of acting
out of old habits we act out of fresh and new insight.
If we cannot find the inner courage needed for this
then we share in the lie which keeps the annual
Christmas festival something void of real meaning,
and we celebrate it without any true feeling. Do we
really rise to the highest concerns of humanity
when we give and receive presents at Christmas
each year out of habit? ... We should forbid ourselves from perpetuating this inner hollowness of

Christmas celebration. We should make the inner decision to imbue this festival with true and worthy content, one which raises humanity to the meaning of its existence. Ask yourselves, my dear friends, whether the feelings in your hearts and souls when you stand before the Christmas tree and open the presents given out of habit, and the Christmas cards containing the same tired phrases—ask yourselves whether feelings are living in you that can raise mankind to an understanding of the sense and meaning of its evolution on earth! All the trouble and sorrow of our times is due to the fact that we cannot find the courage to lift ourselves above the empty phrases of our age. But it must happen. A new content must fill us, one that can give us entirely new feelings that stir us to the depths, as early Christians were stirred in the first centuries AD. These people knew that the Mystery of Golgotha and the appearance of Christ on earth was the highest that human beings could experience. Our souls must once again acquire something of this spirit ...

To this end it is really essential that people help one another in love, so that a real community of souls arises in which envy and all such things disappear, and in which we do not look each at our own particular goal, but face together, united in love, the great goal that we have in common. The

Mystery which the Christmas Child brought into the world embodies this desire to look at a goal in common, without discord among us. The common goal implies union and harmony. The light of Christmas should shine as a light of peace, a light that brings outward peace only because it first sheds inner peace into human hearts. We should understand this and say together: 'Let us realize this and work together with love. Then and only then will we understand Christmas.'

CHRISTMAS AND THE EARTH

4. Old Christmas Play Traditions

Extract from a lecture given in Berlin on
19 December 1915

Here Steiner speaks of the reverent mood of soul that used to surface in rural communities as Christmas approached. The Oberufer Christmas plays, recorded by Karl Julius Schroer, which Steiner revived and made part of the Waldorf School tradition, have a simplicity and humour but also depth of reverence that recalls the profound faith of much older times.

Only a few of these so-called Paradise Plays have remained, which were performed at Christmas and presented the story of Creation. They remained connected to the Shepherds' Play and that of the Three Kings who bring their gifts. Much of this used to live in numerous Christmas plays, but to a large extent they have now disappeared ... These Christmas plays, hand-written, remained in the hands of certain families in the villages and were treasured as something especially sacred. When October came around, people began thinking about having to perform these plays during the Christmas season for the people in the village. Then the best-behaved lads and lasses were chosen and they began to prepare themselves. They were forbidden to drink wine or any alcoholic beverages, or — something which could well happen in such places of course — to be rowdy and dissolute on Sundays, or commit any other transgressions. They really had to lead a 'holy life'. Thus people were aware that a certain moral mood of soul had to be acquired by those who were going to devote themselves to the performance of such plays during the Christmas season. Such plays were ... performed with all the rustic naivety of peasants, and yet the whole thing was imbued with profound, infinite seriousness.

5. Earth Holds Its Breath

Extract from a lecture given in Dornach on
31 March 1923

*In the yearly cycle of the seasons Christmas comes at a
time when the earth is most separate and distinct from the
cosmos, most alone with itself — like someone who has
breathed in and holds his breath. By analogy one can also
say that this midwinter period corresponds to the 'midnight hour' in the cycle of day and night. Of course we
can 'sleep' through this period like the rest of dormant
nature, but as human beings we also have the opportunity
to awaken at this time to our inmost depths, unsustained
by the physical realities of external warmth and light.*

Today let us consider this seasonal cycle of the earth
as a kind of mighty breathing process which the
earth carries out in relation to the surrounding
cosmos ... Of course it is not air that is breathed in
and out but rather those forces which are at work,
for example, in vegetation — those forces which
push the plants out of the earth in spring and
withdraw again into the earth in autumn, allowing

the green plants to fade and finally paralysing plant growth ...

Let us first look at the earth at the time of the winter solstice, in the last third of December. At this time of year we can compare the earth's breathing with that of a person who has inhaled a breath of air and holds it in his lungs. In the same way the earth holds within itself those forces I spoke of as being inhaled and exhaled. At the end of December it holds these forces within itself. And what is happening then with the earth I can outline for you schematically in the following way ... We can of course only consider one part of the earth in connection with this breathing. We shall consider that part where we ourselves dwell; conditions are of course reversed in the southern hemisphere. We must picture the earth's respiration in such a way that one region exhales while the opposite region inhales ...

Picture the time of December. At the end of December the earth has breathed in fully and holds within itself the forces I referred to. It has entirely sucked in its soul element, for that is what these forces are. It has drawn this completely into itself in the same way that someone holds breath in himself when he inhales.

This is the time when, for good reason, the birth of Jesus is celebrated, because Jesus is thus born out of an earth force containing the entire soul element of the earth within it ...

At Christmas time it has breathed these forces in; it holds its breath. If Jesus is born at this time he is born when the earth is, in a certain sense, not speaking with the heavens, a time when the earth has entirely withdrawn into itself. Jesus is born, then, at a time when the earth spins through cosmic space quite alone, when it is not emitting its breath to be suffused and interwoven by the force of the sun, by the sun's light. At this time of year the earth does not offer up its soul to the cosmos but instead has sucked it inwards into its interiority. Jesus is born on the earth at a time when the earth is alone with itself, isolated as it were from the cosmos.

6. Music and Form: Midsummer to Midwinter

Extract from a lecture given in Dornach on 7 April 1923

Continuing and enlarging the idea of the earth's seasonal cycle as a great rhythm of inhalation and exhalation, Steiner here juxtaposes the two solstice 'moments' of midwinter and midsummer, and characterizes their very different effects on human beings of ancient times who still lived in much closer intimacy with natural rhythms than we do today. In describing midsummer as a time of poetry, music and dancing, in which people went 'out' of themselves to experience a higher sense of their humanity, and midwinter as a time when they experienced the sculptural forces of the earth and became more inwardly aware of the human form, Steiner offers an illuminating polarity. Music and sculptural form as, alternately, more fluid and more solidified opposites – like flowing and freezing water or exhalation and inhalation – are two equally vital ends of a scale and simultaneously harbour their own inherent dangers: of fixity and isolation, on the one hand, and evaporating dissolution on the other. Elsewhere Steiner speaks of these same forces as those of

'Ahriman' and 'Lucifer'; and we can assume that these two extremes are challenges which we meet and need to redress at midwinter and midsummer. To enter too deeply into the nature of earth at midwinter without the renewing force of Christ would leave us imprisoned in physical chains. Between midwinter and midsummer, of course, stands Easter's Cross of Golgotha,[2] its two arms seeming to hold the balance at the time of the equinox. In autumn the archangel Michael likewise holds the balance and is often depicted holding a pair of scales.[3]

In stating that human beings of ancient times came to an understanding of animal and human form at midwinter, Steiner also hints at the crib scene so familiar to us: ox, ass and the archetypal representative of our highest humanity.

Among these ancient forms of consciousness was a most singular one, paradoxical as it may sound to modern people. With the coming of October an urge for some sort of activity began to stir in people's limbs. In the summer, people had to accommodate the movements of their limbs to the demands of agricultural labour; they had to put their hands to the plough, and adapt themselves to external needs. But when the harvest had been gathered in, and their limbs were rested, a need stirred in them for some other kind of activity, and there awoke in them a longing to model, knead and form shapes. We might say that just as an intensive urge had arisen at the time of the St John's festival[4] for dancing and music so towards Christmas an intense urge arose to knead and model, to create forms using any kind of pliant substance available in nature. People had an especially sensitive feeling, for example, for the way water begins to freeze. This gave them the specific impetus to push it this way or that way, so that the ice forms appearing in the water assumed certain shapes. People actually went so far as to keep their hands in the water while ice shapes formed, so that their hands grew numb! In this way, when the water froze under the waves their hands formed, it assumed the most remarkable, artistic shapes— which naturally melted away again.

In our more intellectual age nothing remains of all this except, at most, the custom of lead casting on New Year's Eve, in which molten lead is poured into water and the shapes which arise are interpreted as a forecast for the coming year. But this is the last, abstract remnant of those wonderful activities arising from the human being's inward experience of nature's forces and impulses, expressing itself, as I say, in someone thrusting his hand into water as it was freezing, the hand then becoming numb as he tested how the water formed waves, and the freezing water 'answering' with the most remarkable shapes. In this way human beings found their answers to the questions they asked of the earth. Through music and poetry at the height of summer, they turned towards the heavens with their questions, which answered by sending a faint sense of egohood into their dreaming consciousness. In the depths of winter, in contrast, they no longer turned to the heavens to answer their questions, but to the earth, testing what kinds of forms the earthly element can assume. In doing so, they observed that these emerging forms had a certain similarity to those developed by beetles or butterflies . . . From the sculptural form element that they derived from the earth's natural processes there arose in them the intuitive observation that different animal forms are fashioned entirely out of the earthly element. At Christmas the human being understood the forms of animals. And as he worked, exerted his limbs, even jumped into the water and made certain movements, then jumped out and observed how the solidifying water responded, he gained a sense of the form which he himself had as a human being. But this was only at Christmas time, not otherwise. At other times he had a perception only of the animal world and of what pertains to race and blood-relatedness. At Christmas time he penetrated also to the experience of the human form.

In those times of the ancient mysteries, then, just as ego consciousness was mediated from the heavens so a feeling for the human form was conveyed through the medium of earth. At Christmas time the human being learned to know the earth's formative, shaping force, its moulding and sculpting; whereas at St John's time, at the height of summer, he learned to know how the harmonies of the spheres let the ego resound and penetrate into his dream consciousness.

And thus at special festival seasons the ancient mysteries expanded the human being's experience. On the one hand he learned how the environment of the earth extended out into the heavens so that he could be assured that the heavens held his ego or 'I' in their safekeeping, that it rested there. And at Christmas time . . . the earth gave answers to human questioning through sculptural, plastic forms, so that people gradually came to have an interest in the human form. And so it happened that the human being's perception of himself was not acquired just by being human, but by living in close rhythm with the course of the year. In order for him to come to ego consciousness the heavens opened their windows at midsummer; and in order for him to come to consciousness of his human form the earth in a certain way unfolded her mysteries. Thus the human being was intimately linked with the cycle of the year in such a way that his experience of his humanity could only be gained by allowing himself to be elevated to the heavens at the height of summer and allowing himself to sink in winter into the depths of the earth mysteries, the secrets of the earth.

7. Connected to All the Universe

Extract from a lecture given in Berlin on
24 December 1905

Here Steiner urges us to feel our connection with the earth and the surrounding cosmos in ever more distinct and heartfelt ways, and particularly to become aware of the wonderfully healing quality of the great rhythms of nature in contrast to the erratic movements of our own passions and thoughts. The light that prevails at Christmas heralds a distant future when humanity will live at peace with itself.

Today let us bring to mind ... all that the Christmas festival can bring home to our hearts if we regard the science of the spirit not as a dull, grey theory, not as a mere outward confession, not as a philosophy, but as the very pulse of life within us. Nowadays we live as strangers within nature—far more than we realize ...

The festivals have become abstractions, matters of indifference to modern people. The word today is often something we swear allegiance by or sow discord with, failing to recognize its original significance and power. Yet the alphabetical word ought to be the representative, the symbol of the Word creative in nature around us and in the whole universe—and within us too when self-knowledge awakens. All human beings can become aware of this through the seasons and cycles of nature. It was for this that the festivals were originally established...

Christmas is not a festival of Christendom only. In ancient Egypt, in the regions we ourselves inhabit, and in Asia thousands and thousands of years before the Christian era, we find that a festival was celebrated on the days now dedicated to the celebration of the birth of Christ.

What was the character of this festival which, since time immemorial, has been celebrated all over the world on the same days of the year? Wonderful fire festivals were celebrated in ancient times among the Celts in Scandinavia, Scotland and England, by their priests the Druids. What were they celebrating? They were celebrating the time when winter draws to its close and signs of spring slowly begin to appear. It is quite true that Christmas falls while it is still winter, but nature is already heralding a victory which we can celebrate in a festival of hope, confidence and faith—to use words connected in nearly every language with the

Christmas festival. There is confidence that the sun, again in the ascendant, will be victorious over the opposing powers of nature. We have experienced the days shortening and drawing in as an expression of the dying or rather falling asleep of nature. The days grow shorter and shorter up to the time of the Christmas festival, which our forefathers also celebrated, though in another form. Then the days begin to draw out again and the light of the sun celebrates its victory over the darkness. In our age of materialistic thinking this is an event to which we no longer give much consideration.

In olden times ... the solstice was a personal experience of a higher being — as personal as when some momentous event forces us to come to a vital decision. And it was still more than this. The waxing and waning of the days was not only an expression of an event in the life of a higher being but a sign of something greater still, of something momentous and unique ... Our forefathers felt themselves to be spiritual children of the whole universe and they said: 'We have become human beings through the sun spirit from whom the spirit indwelling us descended. The victory of the sun over darkness commemorates our soul's victory at the time when the sun first shone down upon the earth; when the immortal soul entered the physical body, descending into the darkness of desires, impulses and passions.' ... To those who in olden times were still aware of the human being's living connection with the universe, the victory of the sun signified the great moment when they received the impulse which was essential for their earthly existence, and this great moment was remembered and perpetuated in their festivals.

In all ages, mankind's journey upon the earth has been seen as one whose goal was gradually to draw ever closer to the rhythmic, regular processes of nature. If we think of all that makes up our own inner soul life, and then of the course of the sun and everything connected with it, we are struck by something that it is vital for us to feel and experience: the rhythm and marvellous harmony of natural processes in contrast to the chaos and lack of harmony in our own soul. We all know how rhythmically and with what regularity the sun appears and disappears, how regular and rhythmic all natural processes are which unfold under its influence. Imagine what a stupendous upheaval there would be in the universe if, for a fraction of a second only, the sun were to be diverted from its course. It is only because of this inviolable harmony in the course of the sun that our universe can exist at all, and the rhythmic life processes of all living creatures depend on this harmony. Think of the annual course of the sun; picture to yourselves that it is the sun which charms forth the plants in spring, and then think how difficult it is to imagine the violet flowering out of due season. Seed-time and harvest, everything, even the life of animals, is dependent on the rhythmic course of the sun. Even in the human being everything that is not connected with instincts, passions or with ordinary thinking is rhythmic and harmonious. Think of the pulse or of the process of digestion, and you will sense the mighty rhythm, and marvel at the wisdom implicit in all of nature. Compare with this the irregularity, the chaos of our passions and desires and especially our ideas and thoughts. Think of the regularity of your pulse, your breathing, and then of the irregularity, the erratic nature of your thinking, feelings and will. Yet how wisely the powers of life enable rhythmic forces to prevail over chaos! And how greatly the rhythms of the human body are sinned against by human passions and cravings! Those who have studied anatomy know how marvellously the heart is constructed and regulated, but also what a strain is put upon it by drinking tea, coffee and spirits.

There is wisdom in every part of the divine, rhythmic nature whose very soul is the sun with its regular, rhythmic course ... In earlier times this cosmic harmony was placed as a great ideal before those chosen to be leaders of their fellow human beings. At the sixth stage of initiation a person was called a 'sun hero' or one who 'runs in the paths of the sun' ... Why was this? To reach this level of the ascending ladder of spiritual knowledge such a person needed to have developed an inner life in harmony with the divine rhythms pulsing through the cosmos. His life of feeling and thinking must have rid itself of chaos, of all disharmony, his inner life of soul must beat in perfect accord with the rhythm of the sun in the heavens.

If we think of these people with all their nobility of soul we shall be able to some extent to visualize the future of the human race and the way this future relates to our overall concept of humanity. As humanity is today, many things are settled by majority decisions after much argument and conflict. Wherever such resolutions are still regarded as the ideal, there is no understanding of what truth really is. Where does truth exist in us? It lives in that realm of our being where we think logically. It would be nonsense to decide by a majority vote that $2 \times 2 = 4$ or that $3 \times 4 = 12$. Once we have realized what is true, millions may come and tell us that it is not so, that it is this or that, but we will still have our own inner certainty.

We have reached this point in the realm of scientific thinking, of thinking upon which human passions, impulses and instincts no longer impinge.

Wherever passions and instincts mingle with thinking, people still find themselves involved in strife and dispute, in wild confusion, for the life of instincts and impulses is itself a seething chaos. When impulses, instincts and passions have been purged, however, and transmuted into what is known as Budhi or Chrestos,[5] when they have developed to the level at which logical, dispassionate thinking stands today, when our thinking and feeling have become purified to the extent that what one person feels resonates harmoniously with the feelings of others, then the ideals of ancient wisdom, of Christianity, of anthroposophy,[6] will be realized. It will then be as unnecessary to vote about what is held to be good, ideal and right as it is to vote about what has been recognized as logically right or wrong.

Every human being can place this ideal before his soul, which is also that of the sun hero ... The harmony and regularity with which the sun moves through the seasons, manifesting in the growth of plants and the life of animals, was once also chaos. Harmony was gradually attained at the cost of great travail. Humanity stands today within the same kind of chaos; but out of the chaos there will arise a harmony modelled in the likeness of the harmony of the universe. When this thought takes root in our soul — not as theory, not as doctrine but as living

insight—then we shall feel the full, anthroposophical significance of Christmas. If the 'glory',
the divine revelation of the divine harmony in the
heavenly heights is a real experience within us, and
if we know that this harmony will one day resound
from our own souls, then we can also feel what will
be brought about in humanity itself by this harmony: peace among people of good will. These are
the two feelings which arise at Christmastide; the
great vista of the divine ordering of the world, of
the revelation, the glory of the heavens, can give us
a premonition even now that harmony will one day
prevail in those who open their souls to it. The more
abundantly the harmony of the cosmos fills the
human soul, the more peace and concord will reign
on earth.

The great ideal of peace stands there before us
when we contemplate the course of the sun at
Christmas. When we think about the victory of the
sun over darkness during these days, there is born
in us a great confidence and trust which unites our
own evolving soul with the harmony of the cosmos,
a harmony that does not flow into us in vain. And
then the seed that brings to the earth that peace of
which the religions speak, takes root in us. The
'men of good will' are those who feel this peace. It is
the peace that will spread over the earth when the
same harmony holds sway in our life of feeling that

today exists only in the realm of logic. Strife and discord will then give way to the all-pervading love of which Goethe speaks in his *Hymn to Nature*: 'A single draught from this cup of love will render us impervious to a life of toil and stress.'

In all religions this Christmas festival has been one of confidence, trust and hope, because of a feeling that the light must prevail. Out of the seed planted in the earth something will spring forth which seeks the light and will thrive in the light of the coming year. Just as the seed of the plant is cradled in the earth and matures in the light of the sun, so the divine truth, the divine soul itself is immersed in the depths of the life of passion and instinct; there in the darkness this divine sun soul must grow to maturity ...

The great festivals exist to bear witness to our connection with the whole universe, and to help us use our powers of feeling and thinking in such a way that we become fully aware of this connection. When this insight lives within us, the festivals will change their present character and become living realities in our hearts and souls. They will be points of focus in the year, uniting us with the all-pervading spirit of the universe.

Throughout the year we fulfil the common tasks and duties of daily life, but at these festival times we turn our attention to the links which bind us with eternity. And although daily life is fraught with many a struggle, at these times a feeling awakens within us that above all strife and turmoil peace and harmony reign.

DELVING TO THE CORE

8. Christmas Initiation: Seeing the Sun at Midnight

Extract from a lecture given in Berlin on
17 December 1906

*In this excerpt Steiner describes an ancient initiation rite
that took place at the time of the winter solstice. While
this hearkens back to a pre-Christian age, developing
vision that can penetrate matter and discover spirit active
in and beyond it is still essential for humanity's future
development. The 'sun at midnight' is also an image of
Christ transfiguring the material world; and in fact, as
Steiner says elsewhere in this volume, we can find faint
echoes of such initiation rituals in the Christian midnight
mass.*

[The initiation] took place at the time when darkness on the earth is greatest, when the external sun
gives out least light and warmth: at Christmas
time... At this time of year forces favourable for
such an awakening stream through cosmic space...
The pupil's gaze was directed to the time when our
earth was not as it is now, when there was no sun,

no moon shining in the heavens, but both were still united with the earth; when earth, sun and moon formed one body. The human being was already in existence at that time but had no body, was still a wholly spiritual being ... Then came the time when the sun separated from the earth, when its light shone down upon the earth from without. The sun withdrew from the earth and inner darkness came over the human being. This was the beginning of our evolution towards a future when inner light will again be radiant within us. It was necessary for us to learn to know earthly things with our outer senses, to evolve to the stage where the higher self, the Spirit Self,[7] again glows and shines within us. From light, through darkness, to light—this is the path of human evolution.

After being prepared in this way, pupils of the mysteries were led to their actual awakening. This was the moment when, as chosen ones, their eyes of spirit were opened and they perceived the light of spirit. This sacred moment came when the outer sun was shining with least strength ...

Early in the evening the pupils gathered together, in quiet contemplation ... In deep silence and darkness they sat together. When the midnight hour grew near they had been immersed in darkness for long hours, steeped in the contemplation of eternal truths. Then mysterious tones began to resound, now louder, now gentler, filling the space around them. The pupils knew they were hearing the music of the spheres and their hearts were filled with profound devotion. Then a faint light began to glimmer from an illumined disc ... representing the earth. The illumined disc became darker and darker until finally it was quite black. At the same time the surrounding space grew brighter. Again the pupils knew that the black disc represented the earth; and the sun which otherwise radiates light to the earth is hidden. Then ring upon ring of rainbow colours appeared around the earth disc ... the radiant *Iris*. At midnight, in the place of the black earth disc, a violet-reddish orb gradually became visible, on which a word was inscribed that varied depending on the culture and language of those participating in the mystery. For us the word would be *Christos*. Those who gazed at it knew that this was the sun which appears at the midnight hour when the world around lies at rest in profound darkness. The pupils thus experienced what was known in the mysteries as 'seeing the sun at midnight'.

Those who are truly initiated can perceive the sun at midnight, for in them matter has been extinguished; the sun of the spirit alone lives within them, dispelling with its light the darkness of material existence ... So that pupils might realize this even more intensely, after they had experienced the rising of the spiritual sun, the Christos, they were taken to a cave where there seemed to be nothing but stone, nothing but dead, lifeless matter. But springing out of the stones they saw ears of corn as tokens of life, indicating symbolically that out of apparent death life arises, born from the dead stone . . .

The same truth is indicated in the Gospel of St John in the words: 'He must increase but I must decrease!' John, the herald of the coming Christ, of the spiritual light, whose festival falls at mid-summer,[8] must 'decrease' and in this decreasing grows the power of the coming spiritual light, increasing to the extent that John 'decreases'. The grain of seed likewise must wither and decay so that the new plant may live and grow. It was necessary for pupils of the mysteries to realize that life rests within death, that new flowers and fruits arise and flourish out of decay and death, that the earth teems with the powers of birth. They needed to learn that at this time of year something is happening within the earth: the overcoming of death by life, by the life that is present in death. They felt and experienced this as they watched light growing, shining, conquering the darkness. Then in the cave they beheld life springing up in splendour out of apparent death.

9. Love, the Greatest Power

Extract from a lecture given in Berlin on
24 December 1912

*Here Steiner speaks of love as a central, mediating force
between power and wisdom, and yet as something
essentially different from either of them. There are shadow
sides to both power and wisdom, which recall the polarity
mentioned in the introduction to section 6 between the
forces of Lucifer and Ahriman. But love, in the sense
hinted at here, cannot be corrupted, and only through
such love can we truly approach the Christmas Jesus
child.*

What is it really that we should write in our
thoughts—the feelings we can engender in ourselves on this Christmas Eve?

In this Christmas night there should pour into
our hearts the fundamental human feeling of love,
which says: compared with all other forces, powers
and treasures of the world, the treasure, power and
force of love is the greatest and loftiest. Into our
hearts should pour the feeling that wisdom is a

great thing, but love is still greater; that power is a great thing, but love is still greater. And this feeling of the power, force and strength of love should pour into our hearts so strongly that from this Christmas night something may overflow into all our feelings during the rest of the year. Then our deeds at any time throughout the year would shame us if they fall short of the universal power of love we can pour into our souls on Christmas night ...

Those who can feel that love is higher in nature than power, strength and wisdom have a proper sense and feeling for the Christ impulse. We must strive for wisdom, as spirit-endowed human individuals, for wisdom is an expression of the divine at work in the world ... we must not dispense with wisdom, but cherish it in order to evolve further ...

Through wisdom the world is conceived, seen and illumined. Through power and might the world itself is fashioned and built. Everything that occurs does so through the power and might inherent in the world, and we would be shutting ourselves off from the world if we did not seek a share in its power and might. We see this mighty power in the world when the lightning flashes through the clouds, when thunder rolls or rain pours down to drench the earth, or when the sun's rays stream down to conjure life from plant seeds slumbering in it ...

Between them — between power and wisdom — stands love. We can speak of omnipotence as a kind of ideal, but at the same time this conjures the contrary image of Ahriman.[9] We can speak of omniscience as an ideal, but at the same time this conjures the opposing force of Lucifer ... If we love rightly, though, we cannot speak of 'all-love' for it is incapable of increase. Wisdom can be small, and can increase. Power can be small and can increase. Therefore wisdom and power can stand before us as necessary ideals (albeit ones with inherent dangers). But cosmic love does not allow the concept of all-love, being something unique.

The Jesus child as embodied in the Gospel of St Luke can be felt as the personification of love — placed between omniscience and omnipotence. And we really feel this way because the figure is a child, though more intensely because this child has the quality of forlornness, of being cast into a lonely corner. But omniscience is there too — nothing anywhere in the universe is imbued with such wisdom as the miracle that builds the child's body ... like the very essence of wisdom the child lies there. And the Jesus child, cast out into a remote, desolate corner, seems to us like a picture of perfection, concentrating universal wisdom within himself.

But omnipotence also appears personified when we look on the child as described in the Gospel of St

John ... we need to fully grasp what the divine powers and forces of nature can achieve. Think of the might of the powers of nature when the elements are raging, think of all the brewing of universal powers and forces ... the whirling and raging of it all. And now imagine all this storming and raging of the elements being suspended, held at bay from a tiny spot in the world so that the miraculous edifice of the child's body may lie there: for it must be protected. If it were exposed for one moment to the violence of the powers of nature it would be swept away. This can give you a sense of how the child is immersed in omnipotence. And now you can grasp the feeling that can pass through the soul when it gazes with simple heart on what is expressed in the Gospel of St Luke. Compared with this 'essence of wisdom' in the child the greatest human wisdom is but mockery and foolishness, for it can never be as great as the wisdom that went to create the body of the child before us. The highest wisdom remains foolishness and must stand abashed before the childlike body and pay homage to heavenly wisdom, knowing that it cannot attain it ... No, with wisdom we cannot approach what is placed before us as the Jesus child in St Luke's Gospel. Can we approach him with power?

We cannot approach him with power, for the use of 'power' can only have a meaning where a contrary power comes into play. But the child meets us — however much or little power we use — with his powerlessness, mocking our power with powerlessness ...

That is the wonderful thing, that the Christ impulse, germinal in the Jesus child, meets us in the Gospel of St Luke in such a way that, be we ever so wise, we cannot approach him with wisdom; and nor can we approach him with power. Of all that at other times connects us with the world nothing — neither wisdom nor power — can approach the Jesus child as St Luke's Gospel describes him but love. To bring love towards the child, unlimited love, is the only possible thing. The power of love, and the justification and significance of love and love alone is what we can feel most deeply when we allow the contents of the Gospel of St Luke to work on our soul.

We live in the world, and should not scorn any of its forces and impulses. It would be a denial of our humanity and a betrayal of the gods for us not to strive for wisdom; every day and every hour of the year is well spent in realizing the human mission to grow wiser. And likewise every day and every hour compels us to realize that we are immersed in and imbued with the forces and powers of the world — the omnipotence that pulsates through the world. But there is one moment when we can forget this,

when we remember instead what St Luke's Gospel
places before us: when we think of the child who is
still more imbued with wisdom and still more
powerless than all other children, and before whom
the highest love appears in its full validity, before
whom wisdom and power must fall silent and
still...

And what must be added to wisdom and power
as a third thing and must sink into our souls as
something transcending the other two is presented
to us as the quality and power through which
human evolution proceeds ... And if at Christmas
an understanding of the feeling of love is rightly
awakened in us, if we celebrate this birth of
Christ—the awakening of love—then the moment
in which we experience it can radiate what we need
for the remaining hours and days of the year,
flowing through and blessing the wisdom we continually strive for.

Try to awaken in your souls something of the
feeling that can come over us when we inwardly
realize those impulses of love which must at last, in
the distant and still more distant future, come ever
closer to us, when the Christ impulse ... takes hold
on human evolution with ever-increasing power,
ever-increasing understanding. For it will only take
hold if there are souls who understand its full significance—although in this realm 'understanding'

cannot be devoid of love. Love is the fairest thing in human evolution, to which we give birth in our souls this Christmas Eve when we infuse our hearts with that spiritual picture of the Jesus child, cast out by the rest of humanity, cast in a remote corner, born in a stable. Such is the picture of him given to us—as though he comes into evolution from without, and is received by the simplest in spirit, the poor shepherds.

10. From Paradise to Golgotha: the Thirteen Holy Nights

Extract from a lecture given in Hanover on
26 December 1911

*The fact that our present Christmas festival is focused on
25 December, says Steiner, is due to loss of perception of
what Christmas originally celebrated – not the birth of a
child but the descent of Christ into the body of Jesus at the
Jordan baptism. Yet this shift from 6 January to 25
December also contains a deep, inherent wisdom, which
relates the birth of Jesus to the purity of soul which
humanity possessed before embarking on its earthly
travails. The 13 holy nights between the one date and the
other can be experienced as an arduous journey of the soul
from its past to its future.*

When the candles are lit on the Christmas tree, the
human soul feels as though the symbol of an eternal
reality were standing there, and that this must
always have been the symbol of the Christmas
festival, even in a far distant past. For in the
autumn, when outer nature fades, when the sun's

creations fall as it were into slumber, our organs of outer perception must turn away from the phenomena of the physical world. Then the soul has both the opportunity and the urge to withdraw into its innermost depths in order to feel and experience the inner, spiritual light within. The lights on the Christmas tree stand before us as a symbol of the inner, spiritual light that is kindled in outer darkness. And because we feel the spirit light of the soul shining into the darkness of nature as an eternal reality, we imagine that the illumined fir tree shining out to us on Christmas night must have been shining ever since our earthly incarnations[11] began.

And yet it is not so. It is only one or at most two centuries ago that the Christmas tree became a symbol of the thoughts and feelings which arise in us at the Christmas season. The Christmas tree is a recent symbol, but each year anew it reveals to us a great, eternal truth. That is why we imagine that it must always have existed, even in the remote past. It is as if the Christmas tree itself resounds with divine revelation from cosmic expanses, from heavenly heights. We can feel this to be the soul's unfailing source of peace, issuing from our good will. And this revelation also resounded in the legend of Christmas when the shepherds visited the child whose birth we celebrate on Christmas Day. It rang forth to the shepherds, revealing the divine forces at work in cosmic expanses, in heavenly heights, and bringing unfailing peace to the human soul when it is of good will.

For many centuries people could not believe that the symbolic content of the Christmas festival had ever had a beginning. They felt the hallmark of eternity in it. Christian ritual has for this reason clothed the eternal quality of what takes place symbolically on Christmas night in the words: 'To us Christ is born anew!' It is as though every year the soul is called upon to feel anew a reality which, it seems, could only have happened once. The eternity of this symbolic event is brought home to us with infinite power if we have a true feeling for the symbol itself. Yet as late as AD 353, 353 years after Christ Jesus had appeared on earth, the birth of Jesus was not celebrated, even in Rome. The festival of Jesus' birth was celebrated for the first time in Rome in the year AD 354. Before then the day of supreme commemoration for those who under-stood something of the deep wisdom contained in the Mystery of Golgotha was 6 January, not 24 or 25 December. The Epiphany was celebrated as a kind of birth festival of the Christ during the first three centuries of our era. It was a festival to remind human souls of the descent of the Christ spirit into the body of Jesus of Nazareth at the Jordan baptism

by John. Until the year AD 353 this was commemorated on 6 January as the festival of Christ's birth,
for during the first centuries of Christendom an
inkling still survived of the mystery that is of all
mysteries the most difficult for mankind to grasp:
the descent of the Christ being into the body of Jesus
of Nazareth.

What were the feelings of those who had some
inkling of the secrets of Christianity during its first
few centuries? They said to themselves: 'The Christ
spirit is interwoven with the world revealed to us
through the senses and the human spirit.' ... In the
early centuries of Christianity those who understood its true significance cultivated reverence for
the Jordan baptism at which the sun-earth spirit—
the Christ—descended into Jesus of Nazareth. This
birth of Christ was celebrated as a mystery in the
early Christian centuries ... Although what had
actually occurred in the event indicated symbolically by the Jordan baptism was not widely
understood, people nevertheless sensed that the
sun spirit had been born as earth spirit, that a cosmic power had shone out within an earthly human
being. The birth of Christ Jesus in the body of Jesus
of Nazareth, the appearance of Christ on earth, was
celebrated in the early centuries of Christendom on
6 January.

But insight, even dim, uncertain insight into this

deep mystery, faded increasingly as time passed. The age came when people could no longer comprehend that the being called Christ had been present in a physical human body for just three years. What was accomplished for the whole of Earth evolution during those three years in which Christ dwelt in the physical body of a man is one of the most difficult mysteries to understand. From the fourth century onwards the powers of the human soul — which were preparing for the approach of the materialistic age — were not strong enough to grasp this deep mystery. From our own time onwards it will come to be understood ever more clearly. But at that period, as the outer power of Christianity increased, so the inner understanding of the Christ mystery faded. The festival of 6 January ceased to have any essential meaning.[12] The birth of Christ was placed 13 days earlier and envisaged as coincident with the birth of Jesus of Nazareth. But in this very fact we meet something that must always be a source of inspiration and thanksgiving; 24/25 December was fixed as the day of Christ's nativity because a great truth had been lost, as we have heard. And yet such profound meaning lay behind it that — although the people responsible knew nothing of it — we cannot but marvel at the subconscious wisdom with which the festival of Christmas Day was instituted.

Divine wisdom was at work in the fixing of this
festival. Just as divine wisdom can be perceived in
outer nature if we know how to decipher what is
revealed there, so we can perceive it working in
the unconscious human soul when we consider
the following. In the calendar, 24 December is the
day dedicated to Adam and Eve, the next day
being the festival of Christ's nativity. Thus the
loss of an ancient truth caused the date of Christ's
birth to be placed 13 days earlier and to be identi-
fied with the birth of Jesus of Nazareth. But in a
most wonderful way the birth of Jesus of Nazareth was linked with the thought of our origin in
Earth evolution, in Adam and Eve. All the wonderful institutions connected with this festival of
Jesus' birth were alive in the human soul, though
inaccessible to waking consciousness. Such feelings, if one examines them closely, speak a wonderful language.

Understanding was lost for what should have
been celebrated on 6 January—for what streamed
into humanity from cosmic worlds. And yet,
through the hidden forces at work in unconscious
depths, the human soul and spirit was presented to
humanity in the form in which it descends into the
physical body, as the child at the beginning of
physical evolution on earth. But this is not a human
child in the ordinary sense; it is the child who was

there before human beings had reached the point of the first physical embodiment in Earth evolution. This is the being known in the Kabbalah as Adam Cadmon — the human being who descended from divine, spiritual heights with all that he acquired during the periods of Saturn, Sun and Moon incarnation.[13] The human being in his spiritual state at the very beginning of earth evolution, born in the Jesus child — this was what divine wisdom presented to humanity through the festival of Jesus' birth. At a time when it was no longer possible to understand what had descended to earth from cosmic worlds, from heavenly spheres, remembrance was engraved into human souls of their origin, of their state before the advent of the luciferic forces[14] in Earth evolution. It was no longer understood that at the baptism by John in the Jordan there had come into human souls the self-revealed power of the divine, so that peace might reign among people of good will; yet when this event could no longer be understood or celebrated, another affirmation was presented in its place — that at the beginning of Earth evolution, before the luciferic forces began their work, we possessed an unsullied nature and being, which can inspire us with undying hope.

The Jesus of the Gospel of St Luke — not the Jesus described in the Gospel of St Matthew — is the child before whom the shepherds worship, hearing in their souls the words of divine revelation from heavenly heights that bring peace to people of good will. This festival came about for the centuries in which a higher reality was beyond human understanding; it is one which reminds us each year that although we may not be able to gaze into the heavenly heights and recognize the sun spirit, yet we bear within us, from the time of our earthly beginning, a pure child soul, unsullied by the effects of physical incarnation. The forces of this child soul can give us the firm confidence that we can be victorious over the lower nature which clings to us as the result of Lucifer's temptation. The festival of Jesus' birth was linked with remembrance of Adam and Eve to show that at the place visited by the shepherds a human soul had been born in the state of innocence in which the soul existed before the first incarnation on earth.

Since the birth of the God was no longer understood, human birth was commemorated at this festival. For however much our forces threaten to decline and our sufferings gain the upper hand, there are two unfailing sources of peace, harmony and strength. We are led to the first source when we look out into cosmic space, knowing it to be pervaded by the weaving life, movement and warmth of divine spirit. When we hold fast to the conviction that this divine, spiritual power weaving through the universe can permeate our being, if we do not allow our strength to fail, we have the Easter thought: a source of hope and confidence flowing to us from the cosmic spheres. The second source can spring from the dim inkling that as a being of soul and spirit, before we became the prey of luciferic forces at the beginning of earthly evolution, we were still part of the very same spirit which, in the Easter thought, we look towards cosmic worlds to find. Turning to the source to be found in our own, original being before the onset of the luciferic influence, we can say to ourselves: 'Whatever may befall you, whatever may torment you and draw you down from the shining spheres of the spirit, your divine origin is an eternal reality, hidden though it be in the depths of the soul. Recognition of this innermost power of the soul will give birth to the firm assurance that the heights are within your reach. And if you conjure before your soul all that is innocent, childlike, free from life's temptations, free from all that has already befallen human souls through many incarnations since the beginning of earthly evolution, then you will have a picture of the human soul as it was before these earthly incarnations began.'

But one soul — one soul only — remained in this condition, the soul of the Jesus child described in the Gospel of St Luke. This soul was kept back in worlds of spirit when the other human souls began to pass through their incarnations on earth. This soul remained in the guardianship of the holiest mysteries through the Atlantean and post-Atlantean epochs until the time of the events in Palestine. Then it was sent forth into the body predestined to receive it and became one of the two Jesus children[15] — the child described in the Gospel of St Luke.

Thus did the festival of Christ's descent become the festival of the birth of Jesus. What we believe to be born anew symbolically every Christmas Eve is, rightly understood, the human soul in its original nature, our childhood spirit as it was at the beginning of Earth evolution when it descended as a revelation from heavenly heights. And when the human heart can become conscious of this reality, the soul is filled with the unshakeable peace that can bear us to our lofty goals if we are of good will. Mighty indeed is the word that can resound to us on Christmas night if we can truly understand it.

Why was it that the festival of Christ's birth was set back 13 days and became the festival of the birth of Jesus? To understand this we must penetrate into deep mysteries of human existence. Of outer nature we believe, because we see it with our eyes, that what the rays of the sun charm forth from the depths of the earth, unfolding into beauty through the spring and summer, withdraws into those same depths at the time when the outer sun is weakest, and that what will spring forth again the following year is being prepared in the seeds deep within the earth. Because our eyes bear witness we believe that the seed of the plant passes through a yearly cycle, that it must descend into the earth's depths in order to unfold again under the warmth and light of the sun in spring. But we do not so readily understand that the human soul, too, passes through such a cycle. Nor is this revealed until we can be initiated into the great mysteries of existence. Just as the force contained in the seed of every plant is bound up with the physical forces of the earth, so is the inmost being of the human soul bound up with the spiritual forces of the earth. At the time we know as Christmas, the human soul descends into deep, deep spirit realms, drawing strength from these depths as does the seed of the plant for its blossoming in spring. What the soul undergoes in these spirit depths of the earth is entirely hidden from ordinary consciousness. But for one whose eyes of spirit are opened, the 13 days and 13 nights between 24 December and 6 January are a time of deep spiritual experience.

Parallel with the experience of the plant seed in the depths of the natural earth there is a spiritual experience in the earth's spirit depths — truly a parallel experience. And the seer for whom this experience is possible, either as the result of training or through inherited clairvoyant faculties, can feel himself penetrating these spiritual depths. During this period of the 13 days and nights, the seer can behold what must come upon us because we have passed through incarnations under the influence of the forces of Lucifer since the beginning of earthly evolution. The sufferings in kamaloca[16] that we must endure in the world of spirit because Lucifer has been at our side since we began to incarnate on the earth — the clearest vision of all this is to be found in the mighty imaginations that can dawn on the soul during the 13 days and nights between the Christmas festival and 6 January, the Epiphany. At the time when the seed of the plant is passing through its most crucial period in the earth's depths, the human soul is also passing through its deepest experiences. The soul gazes at a vista of all that we must experience in the worlds of spirit because, under Lucifer's influence, we alienated ourselves from the creating powers of the cosmos. This vision is clearest to the soul during these 13 days and nights, preparing it in the best way for the appearance of what may be called the Christ imagination. This can make us aware that by gaining victory over Lucifer, Christ himself becomes the judge of the deeds of human beings during the incarnations affected by Lucifer's influence. From the festival of Jesus' birth to that of the Epiphany, the soul of the seer experiences a revelation of the Christ mystery. It is during this time that the soul can most deeply grasp the full meaning and significance of the Jordan baptism by John...

Many a seer — either schooled in modern spiritual perception or possessing inherited powers of clairvoyance — tells us how at the darkest point of the winter solstice the soul can have vision of all that we must undergo because of our alienation from the Christ spirit, how redemption and catharsis were made possible through the mystery enacted in the baptism by John at the Jordan and then through the Mystery of Golgotha; and how the visions during the 13 nights are crowned on 6 January by the Christ imagination. Thus it is correct to name 6 January as the day of Christ's birth, and these 13 nights as the time during which clairvoyant powers in the human soul discern and perceive what must be undergone in the incarnations leading from Adam and Eve to the Mystery of Golgotha.

During my visit to Christiania [now Oslo] last year, I was struck to find these thoughts ... embodied in a beautiful saga known as the Dream Legend. It has surfaced in Norway in the last 10 to

15 years and has become very well known, although it dates back to much older times. This legend relates in a wonderful and beautiful way how Olaf Åsteson is initiated, as it were by natural forces; he falls asleep on Christmas Eve, sleeps through the 13 days and nights until January 6, and lives through all the terrors that the human being must experience through incarnations from the earth's beginnings until the Mystery of Golgotha. And it tells how, when 6 January comes, Olaf Åsteson has a vision of the intervention of the Christ spirit in humanity, the Michael spirit being his forerunner and herald ...

The Christmas thought, if we understand the festival which commemorates man's divine origin and the symbol before us on Christmas day in the form of the Jesus child, repeatedly tells us that we can find within ourselves the powers which bring peace to the soul. True peace of soul is present only when the peace has sure foundations, when it is a force enabling us to know that something lives in us which, if truly brought to birth, can and must lead us to divine heights and powers.

The lights on this tree are symbols of the light that shines in our own souls when we grasp the reality which the Jesus child, in his state of innocence, proclaims to us symbolically on Christmas Eve: the inmost being of the human soul itself, innocent, tranquil, leading us along our life's path to the highest goals of existence. May these lights on the Christmas tree say to us: 'If ever your soul is weak and you feel your goals are beyond your reach, think of the human being's divine origin and become aware of those forces within you which are also the forces of supreme love. Exert your greatest strength to become inwardly conscious of the forces that will give you confidence and certainty in all that you do, throughout life, now and in all ages of time to come.'

11. Extract from the Dream Song of Olaf Åsteson

Below is a small excerpt from the ancient Norwegian epic mentioned by Steiner in the previous lecture, evoking an inner journey of initiation between 25 December and 6 January.

I laid me down in the Holy Night
Deep sleep upon me fell.
I wakened not till the thirteenth day
When folk to church did go.
   The moon shone brightly
   And far ahead the ways led.

Lo I have been in cloudy heights
And deep in ocean depths;
And whosoe'er will follow me,
No laughter gladdens his lips.
   The moon shone brightly
   And far ahead the ways led.

Lo I have been in cloudy heights
And deep in miry sloughs,
And I have seen the blaze of hell
And one part seen of heaven

> The moon shone brightly
> And far ahead the ways led ...

The hound he bites, the serpent stings,
The bull sets to his horns,
They suffer none to cross the bridge
Who have condemned without cause
> The moon shone brightly
> And far ahead the ways led ...

I had to wade through Murkmire Moor
My feet no ground could find.
And so I passed from the Gjallard Bridge
The dust of death in my mouth.
> The moon shone brightly
> And far ahead the ways led ...

So went I on my winter way
That lay at my right hand;
And lo, I saw there paradise
Its light shed o'er that fair land.
> The moon shone brightly
> And far ahead the ways led.

God's Holy Mother there I saw,
No wonder could be more fair.
'To Brooksvalin now wend thy way,
there judgement shall be given.'
> The moon shone brightly
> And far ahead the ways led ...

THE CHILD AND THE TREE

12. The Jesus Child

Extract from a lecture given in Berlin on
21 December 1911

Many traditional legends tell of nature flourishing at midwinter to greet the birth of Jesus. Here Steiner relates such stories to the profound renewal which the Mystery of Golgotha signified for the earth.

As long as humanity underwent its descent into matter and all that the forces of heredity entailed throughout the generations up to the Mystery of Golgotha, so long had it been absorbing destructive forces that entered right into the blood. A single soul had remained behind in worlds of spirit ... and then entered humanity as the soul of the Jesus child described by the Gospel of St Luke ...

Why then was the divine child placed before humanity for centuries as the highest aspect one can revere? It is because, when we look at a child and see a being that cannot yet say 'I' to itself, we can nevertheless recognize in this child the signs of his origin in the world of spirit. In this contemplation of child nature we can learn to have full trust in human nature. At this time of year when the sun shines least, when people can rest from their labours, when days are shortest and nights longest, and all external beauty withdraws for a while from view, western civilization places the birth festival of the divine child, of the human being who enters the world pure and unsullied—and who, through his innocent entry into the world can give us the greatest confidence in our divine origin ...

A wonderful thought unites with a wonderful emotion in our souls when we see how in the centuries after the festival of Jesus' birth was transferred to 25 December[17] a feeling of confidence that flowed into human souls, awoken in response to the pure nature of the child. In paintings, in Christmas plays, was depicted how all the realms of nature bow before the Jesus child, before the divine child who is our origin. There is the wonderful picture of the manger with the beasts bowing before this archetypal human being; then also legends such as that of a tree bowing to Mary on her flight with Jesus to Egypt. Traditional legends throughout Europe tell of trees bowing to this great event, or bearing fruit in the holy night. These are all resonant symbols which testify to the fact that the birth of the Jesus child is connected with the whole life of the earth. If we recall what has so often been aired

here, that in ancient times ... people had clairvoyant insight into the divine worlds of spirit, and
how this clairvoyance gradually vanished from
humanity so that it could acquire the self-reliant
ego, if we recall how something like a drying,
desiccation and withering of the old divine forces
occurred and how the Christ impulse introduced
through the Mystery of Golgotha brought a new
water of life to revive these withering forces, then
we can have a still more profound appreciation of
the Christmas legends that relate how the dried up
and withered roses of Jericho sprout and flourish in
the holy night. According to legend they blossom
and unfold on Chistmas Eve in memory of the time
when Mary, carrying the Christ child to Egypt,
stepped over the place where a rose tree was
growing ...

13. The Golden Legend

Extract from a lecture given in Berlin on
17 December 1906

*Steiner was standing beside a candlelit Christmas tree as
he gave the lecture from which the following excerpt is
taken. Here he tells the legend which traces the origin of
the wood of the Cross back to the Garden of Eden, thus
linking a time before the 'Fall' to a time of future
redemption.*

And so in the whole content of the Christmas festival we feel something echoing from primeval
ages. It has come down to us in the imagery of
Christianity. The symbols of Christianity are
reflections of the most ancient symbols of mankind.
The lighted Christmas tree is one of them. It is a
symbol of the tree of paradise which embodies life
and knowledge. Paradise itself signifies the entirety
of material nature, within which grow the trees of
our spiritual nature and of life. Knowledge can only
be won at the cost of life.

There is a legend which gives expression to the

true meaning of the tree of knowledge and the tree of life. Seth[18] stands before the gate of paradise, craving entry. The cherubim guarding the entrance with a fiery sword allow him to pass — a sign of initiation. In paradise Seth finds the tree of life and the tree of knowledge firmly intertwined. The archangel Michael, who stands in the presence of God, allows him to take three grains of seed from this intertwined tree, which stands there as a prophetic picture of mankind's future. Once the whole of humanity has attained initiation and found knowledge it will bear within it not only the tree of knowledge but also the tree of life; and death will be no more. But in the meantime only an initiate may take from this tree the three grains of seed — which symbolize the higher levels of human development. When Adam died Seth placed these three seeds in his mouth, and from them grew a flaming bush. From the wood cut from this bush new sprouts and leaves kept bursting and flourishing. But within the flaming ring of the bush was written: 'I am he who was, who is, who is to be' — in other words what passes through all incarnations, self-renewing and evolving, which descends out of the light into darkness and out of the darkness ascends again into light.

The staff with which Moses performed his miracles was cut from the wood of the bush; the door of Solomon's temple was fashioned from it. The wood was carried to the waters of the pool of Bethesda, and from it the pool received its healing properties. And from this same wood the Cross of Christ Jesus was made, the wood of the Cross which is a symbol of life passing into death, but containing within itself the power to engender new life. Here we see the great universal symbol of life conquering death. The wood of this Cross has grown from the three grains of seed of the tree of paradise.

The rose cross is likewise a symbol of the death of our lower nature and the resurrection of the higher. Goethe expressed this in the words:

As long as you have not grasped
Life issuing forth from death
You're but a troubled guest
Upon the shrouded earth.

The tree of paradise and the wood of the Cross are connected in a most wonderful way. Even though the Cross is always an Easter symbol it deepens our conception of the Christmas mystery too. We feel how in this night of Jesus' nativity, new upwelling life streams towards us. This thought is indicated in the fresh roses adorning our tree. They tell us that the tree of Christmas Eve has not yet become the wood of the Cross, but the power to become that wood is beginning to arise in it. The roses growing out of the green are a symbol of the victory of eternity over time ...[19] The pentagram symbol greeting us from the summit of the tree represents everything which permeates the universe and is centred in the human being ... It is the star of humanity, of evolving humanity. It is the star that all enlightened people follow, as did the wise magi of old. It symbolizes the very essence and meaning of earth existence, the great sun hero who comes to birth in the holy night because the greatest light shines forth then from the deepest darkness. In a future towards which we are striving the light will be born within us. Those significant words 'The darkness comprehended not the light' will be transformed and truth will ring out into cosmic space; then darkness *will* comprehend the light which shines towards us from the star of humanity, will give way to it and comprehend it, that is, be wholly grasped and permeated by it.

The Christmas festival should strike this resounding note within us. Only then do we truly celebrate its deep, original message; only then does it point forwards to the light of spirit which will one day shine out from our inner being, illuminating the whole world. The Christmas festival embodies the highest ideals of mankind. If we can celebrate it truly it will regain life and significance in our souls, and the Christmas tree also, as symbol of the tree of paradise, will take on a truer meaning. Then a joyful assurance will arise in our souls that we, too, will experience the birth of the higher self, that within each one of us will be born the Saviour, the Christ.

14. Innocence and Experience

Extract from a lecture given in Berlin on
19 December 1915

Here Steiner urges us to reconnect with the child in us which, more than the world-weary adult, embodies an unsullied aspect of our highest self, and is ultimately the source of all healing.

The God presented to us in the Old Testament gives one commandment to the human being, represented by Adam and Eve: 'You may eat from all the fruits of the garden; you must avoid only the fruits that grow on the tree of knowledge of good and evil, because they who have eaten of that fruit would be cast out from their original realm of existence.'

The tree however, which was now represented in very diverse ways, came by some means into the sequence of generations from which the physical body of Christ Jesus arose. This was portrayed as follows. When Adam, the fallen human being, was buried, this tree again grew out of his grave and was thus removed from paradise. In this story we see the thought presented that Adam, the human being sundered from paradise, who was tempted by Lucifer, rests in the grave and unites himself with the body of the earth; but out of his grave the tree grows, which can now grow out of the earth with which Adam's body has united.

The wood of this tree passes over to the generations to which Abraham and also David belong. And out of the wood of this tree, which originally stood in paradise and then grew again out of Adam's grave, the Cross was made on which Christ Jesus was crucified.

This is the picture repeatedly portrayed to those pupils who were to be initiated into the secrets of the Mystery of Golgotha. There is a deep meaning in the fact that in ancient times deep thoughts came to expression in such pictures, and this meaning holds good for the present as well. It will become clear to us that it still holds true for us today.

We have also acquainted ourselves with the view of the Mystery of Golgotha that tells us that the being who lived on earth through the body of Jesus poured out over the earth what he could bring to it, poured it into the earth's aura. What the Christ brought into the earth has since then become united with the entire corporeality of the earth. The earth has become something different since the Mystery of Golgotha. What Christ brought out of heavenly heights down to the earth is living in the earth aura.

If we consider this spiritually in connection with the ancient picture of the tree, this picture shows us the entire circumstances from a higher point of view. The luciferic principle entered the human being when he first began earth existence. The human being as he now is in his union with the luciferic principle belongs to the earth, indeed he forms a part of the earth. And when someone dies and his body is laid into the earth, this body is not just as modern anatomy conceives it, but is at the same time the outer form or mould of what the human being is in his inner nature within the earthly realm. Spiritual science can thus show us that what goes through the threshold of death and enters the world of spirit is not the sum total of the human being but that, through all his activity and deeds while alive, the human being is united with the earth. He is really united with it in the same way as the phenomena studied by geologists, mineralogists and zoologists.

It is only when the human being passes through the gateway of death that we can say that his individuality ends the connection uniting him with the earth. Our outer form however, which we surrender in some way to the earth, enters the body of the earth. It bears within it the impress of what the earth has become as a result of Lucifer entering earthly evolution. What the human being achieves on the earth bears the luciferic principle within it and the human corpse invests the aura of the earth with this luciferic principle. It is not only the human being's originating intention that arises or as it were blossoms out of human deeds and activities, but also something that has the luciferic principle intermixed with it. This then is the aura of the earth. And when we now look upon the tree growing out of the grave of the original human being Adam, who was led astray by Lucifer, if we look at the tree that has become something different through the luciferic temptation—this tree that was originally the tree of the knowledge of good and evil—we see everything that the human being brought about by the fact that he left his original state of existence, that he became something different through the luciferic temptation and that something was thereby introduced into earthly evolution that was not previously intended.

We see the tree grow out of what forms the human physical body for the earth, whose earthly form became permeated and impressed with what causes us to appear on earth in a lower sphere than we would have done had we not passed through the luciferic temptation. Something grows out of our entire human existence that has entered human evolution through Lucifer's temptation. When we seek knowledge we seek it in a different way than was originally predestined. This makes it seem that something different grows out of our earthly deeds than would accord with the gods' original intention. We form an earthly existence that is not as the gods originally intended for us; we mix something else into it, and we must form very precise pictures of this if we wish to understand it. Definite mental images are required if we wish to grasp it fully and properly.

We have to say to ourselves: 'I am placed into earthly evolution. What I give to earthly evolution through my deeds bears fruit; it bears the fruit of knowledge that has become mine by the fact that I have gained the knowledge of good and evil on the earth. This knowledge lives in the evolution of the earth, is active and present there. As I look at this knowledge however it becomes something different for me, different from what it originally should have been. It becomes something that I must change if the goal and task of the earth are to be achieved. I see growing out of my earthly deeds something that must become different. The tree grows forth, the tree that becomes the Cross of earthly existence, the tree that becomes something to which the human being must gain a new relationship ...

We know that the highest member of our human

nature is the 'I' or ego.[20] We learn to express our 'I' at a definite moment in childhood. We gain a relationship to this 'I' at the point we remember back to in later life — our earliest memory. We know from the most varied findings of spiritual science that until this point the 'I' itself is active, forming and structuring us. This remains the case until the point at which we begin to have a conscious relationship to the ego or 'I'. In the infant this 'I' is also there, but it first works within; its first task is to form our body. To begin with it creates our super-sensible forces in the spiritual world. When we have gone through conception and birth it still works creatively on our body for a period of time that lasts a few years until our body has become a tool enabling us to consciously comprehend ourself as an ego.

A deep mystery is connected with the entry of the 'I' into human bodily nature. When we meet a person we may ask him how old he is and he will give his age as the number of years that have passed since his birth. As has been said we touch here on a certain mystery of spiritual science that will gradually become clearer in the course of time. Today however I only want to touch on it. The age a person considers himself to be at any point in his life is connected with his physical body. He is really just saying that his physical body has been developing for such and such a period since his birth. The 'I' does not go along with this development of the physical body. The 'I' remains as it was.

This is a difficult mystery to grasp, that the 'I' stays at the point of time we remember back to in childhood. It does not change with the body but stays as it is. It is for this very reason that we always have it before us so that, as we look, it can mirror our experiences for us. The 'I' does not take part in our earthly journey. Only when we have gone through the gateway of death must we take the path that we call kamaloca[21] backwards again to our birth in order to encounter our 'I' again and to take the I along with us in our further journey. The 'I' remains behind as we grow up. The body pushes itself forward in years while the 'I' remains behind and stays as it is. This is difficult to understand because one cannot imagine that something remains standing in time as time keeps moving. But this is in fact the case. The 'I' does not actually unite itself with what approaches the human being from earthly existence. It remains united with those forces we call ours in the world of spirit ...

The 'I' is retained in the world of spirit. It must be held back there for otherwise we would never be able to achieve, once more, the earth's original goal and aim as human beings during our earthly evolution. What the human being undergoes here on earth because of his Adam nature, you could say, of which he takes an impress into the grave when he dies as Adam, clings to the physical body, etheric body and astral body[22] and derives from these. The 'I' waits, waits with everything composing it, waits for the entire period of a human being's life on earth until he passes through death and retraces his path to rejoin it and develop further. This means, quite specifically, that we remain with our 'I' in the world of spirit. Humanity should become aware of this fact, and is in fact only able to do so because Christ descended out of those worlds to which the human being belongs, from worlds of spirit. In the body of Jesus he prepared for himself in a twofold way[23] what was to serve him as body on the earth.

If we understand ourselves correctly we always look back through our entire earthly life, back to our childhood. Our spiritual element has remained behind in our childhood. We always look towards this if we wish to understand things properly. And humanity needs to learn to look towards what the spirit in the heights can tell us: 'Suffer the little children to come unto me.' Not adults, who are connected with the earth but, rather, little children...

The Christmas festival shows how Christ prepared the human body for himself during childhood. This is what should give the foundation of the

Christmas experience: knowing how the human being has remained connected with what approaches, now, from what remained behind as we grew up, from the heavenly heights. In the form of the child the human being should be reminded of the human-divine element from which we distance ourselves on descending to the earth, and which has now returned to us. We should be reminded of this childlike element in us, and of him who returned the childlike element to us ...

Let us look for the origin of those impulses that oppose each other in the world today in such an appalling way.[24] Where do these impulses originate? Where does everything originate that makes the life of humanity so difficult today? Where is the origin of all this? It lies in everything we become in the world only after the point in time when we can recollect ourselves. If we go back beyond this point of time, to our state when we were the 'little children who can enter the kingdom of heaven' this is not where it originates. At that point nothing of what today is in battle and dispute resides in human souls. The thought can be expressed this simply, but spiritually we must consider the fact that there is something so original in the human soul that it goes beyond all human strife and disharmony ... There is something that fundamentally unites us with the true Christ thought: we can have moments in our life in which, despite everything we become in the external world, we can bring alive in us what we received as a child. We can do this by going backwards, feeling our way back to the child's view. We can do this by looking towards the human being as he develops between birth and death so as to sense within us what we received as a child ... It is actually true that what existed in childhood remains more alive in some people than others. And this is generally the secret of many great human beings, that right into their oldest age they can remain children in a certain way; even when they die they die as children, though this is only partly true since one also needs to connect fully with life ...

If there are more and more people who come to know how to conceive of Christmas in such a spiritual-scientific sense, this Christmas night will develop a force in human hearts and souls that will have its meaning in all times. It will have meaning in times in which people surrender themselves to feelings of joy but also in times in which people have to surrender themselves to the feelings of pain that must penetrate us today when we think of the great misery of our time ... What can be healing for humanity can develop only if people do not forget that there was not only one Christmas but that there must be an everlasting Christmas, an everlasting coming to birth of the divine spiritual in the physical, earthly human being ...

TOWARDS A NEW CHRISTMAS

15. Past, Present and Future

Extract from a lecture given in Basel on
26 December 1921

Warm feelings of community no longer sustain us, says Steiner; and harking back to a pre-lapsarian state, embodied in the image of the babe in the manger, is no longer enough. We need to develop an understanding of the supersensible nature of Christ that can underpin a new grasp of our own human nature.

In marvellous abundance people have poured out love through the centuries to the Jesus child in the manger. And it is really wonderful to find how strongly this power of love is reflected in the Christmas plays which have come down to us from earlier centuries of Christendom. If we let these things work on us we shall realize how deeply Christmas is a festival of remembrance. We shall realize too that just as the peoples of the Old Testament strove in wisdom to be gathered to the Fathers, so the people of the New Testament have striven in devotion and love to gather

together at Christmas around the sinless child in
the manger.

But who will deny that the love poured out to the
source of Christendom by so many hearts has little
by little become more or less a habit? Who will deny
that in our age the Christmas festival has lost the
living power it once possessed? The people of the
Old Testament longed to return to their origin, to be
gathered to their Fathers, to return to their ances-
tors. The Christian turns his mind and heart to
human nature in its primal purity when he celebrates the festival of the birth of Jesus. And it was
this same Christian instinct which causes human
beings to associate the Christmas festival with their
earthly origin, which led the day before Christmas,
24 December, to be dedicated to Adam and Eve.
The day of Adam and Eve preceded the day of the
birth of Jesus. And so it was out of a deep instinct
that the tree of paradise came to be associated as a
symbol with the Christmas festival ...

Yet all this has, in another sense, tended to
obliterate the fundamental conception of Christianity. No one nowadays can fail to realize that
people have little insight into the Godhead as not
only Father Principle but also as *Son.* Humanity in
general — as well as our supposedly enlightened
theologians — has more or less lost sight of the difference between the Father God and the Son God ...

When people today speak of Christ they still associate certain memories of the holy story with his name, but they have no clearly defined feeling of the difference in nature between the Son God on the one hand and the Father God on the other. But at the time that the Mystery of Golgotha made its incisive mark on earthly evolution this feeling was still very much alive. Over in Asia, in a place of no great importance to Rome at the time, Christ had appeared in Jesus of Nazareth. According to the early Christians, Christ was the divine being who had ensouled a human being in a way that had never before occurred on earth, nor would ever occur again. This one event of Golgotha, this one ensouling of a human being by a divine being, by the Christ, imparts meaning and purpose to the whole of earthly evolution. All previous evolution is to be thought of as preparatory to this event of Golgotha, and all subsequent evolution as its fulfilment.

This event took place in Asia; and on the throne of Rome sat Augustus Caesar. People nowadays no longer realize that Caesar Augustus on the throne of Rome was regarded as a divine incarnation. The Roman Caesars were regarded as gods in human form.

And so we have two different conceptions of God. The one upon the throne of Rome and the other on Golgotha, the 'place of a skull'. There could be no greater contrast! Think of the figure of Caesar Augustus who, according to his subjects and according to Roman decree, was a god incarnate in a man. He was thought to be a divine being who had descended to the earth, the divine forces uniting with birth forces, with the blood. Having come down into earthly existence this divine power was seen as pulsing in and through the blood ... People thought of the Godhead as bound up with the forces of the blood and expressed this in the words *Ex Deo nascimur* — we are born out of God. And even the least elevated felt themselves connected with what lived, as the crown of humanity, in an individual like Caesar Augustus.

Everything honoured and revered in this way was a divine Father principle for it was living in the blood which the human being receives as a gift of birth. But at the Mystery of Golgotha the divine Christ being united himself with the man Jesus of Nazareth — not in this case with the stream of inheritance or bloodline, but with the highest forces of the human soul. A God united with a human being in such a way that humanity was saved from falling victim to and being subsumed by the earthly forces of matter.

The Father God lives in the blood. The Son lives in the human soul and spirit. The Father God leads us into material life: *Ex Deo nascimur.* But God the Son lifts us again out of material existence. The Father God leads us from the supersensible into the material. God the Son leads us from the material once more into the supersensible. *In Christo morimur* — In Christ we die ...

Over the course of the centuries, understanding of the risen one, the conqueror of death, has gradually been lost. Enlightened modern theology concerns itself wholly with the *man* Jesus of Nazareth ...

And transcending both birth and death there is a third principle, proceeding from and co-equal both with the divine Father and the divine Son: the Spirit, the Holy Spirit. Within the human being, therefore, we can find the transition from the supersensible to the material, and from the material once again to the supersensible; but we can also find both united in the principle that knows neither birth nor death, by awakening in and through the Holy Spirit — *Per spiritum sanctum reviviscimus.*

For many centuries Christmas was a festival of remembrance. How much of the substance of this festival has been lost is proved by the fact that, for enlightened theology, all that is left of the being Christ Jesus is the man Jesus of Nazareth. But for us today Christmas must become a call and summons to something new. A new reality must be born.

Christianity needs an impulse of renewal, for it no longer understands the Christ being in Jesus of Nazareth, and has therefore lost its meaning and purpose. The meaning and essence of Christianity must be rediscovered. Humanity must once again learn to see that the Mystery of Golgotha can be understood only in the light of supersensible knowledge.

Another factor, too, contributes to this lack of understanding of the Mystery of Golgotha. We can look with love to the babe in the manger, but we have no wisdom-filled understanding of the union of the Christ being with the man Jesus of Nazareth. Nor can we look up into the heavenly heights with the same intensity of feeling that was present in those who lived at the time of the Mystery of Golgotha. At that time people looked up to the starry worlds and saw in the courses and constellations of the stars something like a countenance of the divine soul and spirit of the cosmos. They saw the sun as the heart of this divine, spiritual cosmos. And they saw in Christ the inner spiritual essence of the glorious starry heavens. But for modern man the starry worlds and all the worlds of cosmic space have become little more than a product of calculation.

The world has become empty of gods or God. The Christ being, certainly, could never have descended from the universe we investigate nowadays through astronomy and astrophysics, which is so void of God ... But instinctive feelings for the most holy and sacred things have, after all, been preserved throughout the course of history. Many of these feelings and perceptions have weakened, but to those who are willing to look with unprejudiced eyes the old meaning is still discernible. And so we can read something from the fact that at midnight between 24 and 25 December the midnight mass is said in every Christian church. We can read something from this fact when we know that the mass is nothing less than a synthesis of the rites and rituals of the mysteries which led to initiation, to the beholding of the sun at midnight. This institution of the midnight mass at Christmas is an echo of the initiation which enabled the candidate, at the midnight hour, to see the sun at the other side of the earth and thus to behold the universe as one of spirit, to hear the cosmic Word resounding through the cosmos, revealing, through the courses and constellations of the stars, the essential nature of the universe.

Blood sets human beings at variance with one another. Blood fetters to the earthly and material that element in us which descends from heavenly heights. In our century especially, human beings have gravely sinned against the essence of Christianity, returning again instead to the ties of blood. But they must find their way to the being who was Christ Jesus, who does not address himself to the blood but who poured out his blood and gave it to the earth. Christ Jesus is the being who speaks to the soul and spirit, who does not separate and divide but unites, so that peace may arise on earth, through our understanding of the cosmic Word.

A new understanding of the Christmas festival through supersensible knowledge can transform the material universe into spirit before the eyes of the soul, transform it in such a way that the sun at midnight becomes visible and is known in its spiritual nature. Such knowledge brings understanding of the super-earthly Christ being, the sun being who was united with the man Jesus of Nazareth. It can bring understanding too of the unifying peace that should hover over the peoples of the earth. The being of God is revealed in the heights, and through this revelation peace rings forth from the hearts of 'men of good will'.

This is the message of Christmas. Peace on earth flows into unison with the divine light streaming towards the earth. We need something more than a remembrance of Jesus' day of birth. We need to understand and realize that a new Christmas festival must arise, that a new festival of birth must lead on from the present into the immediate future. A new Christ impulse must be born which recognizes the nature of Christ. We need a new understanding of the truth that the divine heavens—the world of spirit—and the physical world of earth are linked to one another, and that the Mystery of Golgotha is the most significant expression of this union. We must understand once again why it is that the midnight hour of Christmas resoundingly calls on us to remember our divine, spiritual origin, to unite in our thoughts the revelations of the heavens with peace on earth.

The holy night must become conviction and reality. It is not enough to give each other presents at Christmas in accordance with ancient custom and habit. The warm feelings which for centuries inspired Christian folk at the time of the Christmas festival have been lost. We need a new Christmas, a new holy night, reminding us not only of the birth of Jesus of Nazareth but bringing a new birth, the birth of a new Christ impulse. In full consciousness we must learn to understand that in the Mystery of Golgotha a supersensible power was made manifest, was revealed within the material earth. We must be fully aware of what resounded instinctively in the mysteries of old, but we must receive this impulse *consciously*. We must learn to understand once more that when the holy night of Christmas becomes a reality to us we can experience the wonderful midnight union between the revelation of the heavens and the peace of earth.

This is the meaning of the words below, which are dedicated to Christmas. They sum up what I have tried to express to you tonight. Founded on an anthroposophical[25] understanding of Christ, they seek to show how we can rediscover the wisdom that once lived instinctively in human beings, a wisdom which, at the time of the Mystery of Golgotha, was still sufficiently preserved to allow the appearance of the Christ being to be celebrated. Today we must once more develop understanding of the Christ as a cosmic being who united himself with the earth. The time when this understanding is accessible to the greatest number of people is that of the period of the cosmic holy night whose approach we await.[26] If we understand these things then the feelings will awaken in us which I have tried to express in the following verse.

See the sun
at deep midnight,
use stones to build
in the lifeless ground.

So find in decline
and in death's night
creation's new beginning,
morning's fresh force.

Let the heights reveal
divine word of gods;
the depths sustain and nurture
the stronghold of peace.

Living in darkness
engender a sun;
weaving in substance
see spirit's bliss.

16. Reverence as a Healing Force

Extract from a lecture given in Dornach on
23 December 1920

*Here Steiner relates contemporary social ills to a lack of
reverence in our observation of nature, and calls on us to
develop new heart forces in everyday life.*

The way must be found again to the Christmas
mystery. We must become as reverent with regard
to external nature as the shepherds were in their
hearts. In inward vision we must become as wise as
were the Magi in their observation of planets and
stars in space. We must develop inwardly what the
Magi developed outwardly. In our relationship
with the external world we must develop what the
simple shepherds of the field developed in their
souls. Then we shall find the way, the right way, to
a deepened experience of Christ, to a loving com-
prehension of Christ; and then we shall find our
way to the Christmas mystery. Then, with the right
thoughts and feelings, we shall be able to place the
crib beside the original tree of paradise, which does

not only tell us of how we enter the world through natural forces, but of how we must be reborn in order to become conscious of our full humanity ...

We live in serious times and we must see clearly that we need to become human again in the true sense ... The social question that confronts humanity is terribly urgent. Fearful things have come about in recent years and social problems are becoming ever more dire—only those who are asleep in their souls can ignore this. European culture is close to the brink of ruin. Nothing can raise it from its chaotic condition unless people manage to develop real humanity in their daily lives. They will not be able to do this unless their feeling is deepened and made inward by an observation of nature in which they grow as reverent as the simple shepherds ... The shepherds heard, through the power of their hearts, the voice announcing that the Godhead was revealed through cosmic breadths, and that by receiving the divine into one's soul peace can come about among 'men of good will' ...

17. Shepherds and Magi: Two Ways of Knowing

Extract from a lecture given in Dornach on
23 December 1920

'Shepherd' knowledge, springing from a close relationship with nature, and 'Magi' knowledge, based on an intimate perception of the motions of the stars, have changed through the centuries into detached scientific observation on the one hand and abstract mathematical calculation on the other. In other words, a warm and inward connection with nature has become cold, external investigation and experimentation, and a clear-sighted, spirit-imbued vision of the surrounding, external cosmos and its meaning has declined into the head's regal isolation. We need to transform these modern ways of knowing once more, says Steiner, into a living science and imaginative perception which do not lose the hard-won objectivity of modern science, but reinvigorate it with a perception of non-material realities.

The Gospels tell of two proclamations of the birth of Christ Jesus. The one proclamation is made to the simple shepherds in the fields, to whom in dream or in some kindred way an angel announces the birth. In this case the event was perceived through inner soul forces of a particular kind, which these shepherds possessed. The other proclamation is made to the Three Kings, the three Magi from the East who, the Gospel tells us, follow the voice of a star announcing to them that Christ Jesus has come into the world.

Here we have an indication of two ways in which higher knowledge came to people of earlier times... Echoes of ancient wisdom survived here and there in certain exceptional individuals. Such individuals might well have been simple shepherds in the fields whose devout purity of heart possessed a certain power of clairvoyance which came over them like a dream. They could equally have been individuals who had reached the heights of learning, like the three Magi from the East, in whom the ancient faculty to gaze into the flow of cosmic events had been preserved.

In a kind of dream condition the simple shepherds in the fields were able to have an inner vision of what was drawing near in the event of the birth of Christ Jesus. The three Magi from the East, on the other hand, drew upon their knowledge in order to understand the phenomena of the heavens; by so doing they could become aware of a significant event taking place on earth, one far transcending the ordinary.

Our attention is therefore directed to two definite but quite distinct forms of knowledge ... The Magi were able to read the secrets of the movements of the stars. The story points to an ancient lore of the stars, an ancient knowledge of the secrets of the world of stars which could also reveal the secrets of human existence ... People sought in the stars for explanations of what was happening on earth. But to them the world of stars was not the mechanical abstraction it has now come to be. Every planet was felt to have a reality of *being*. In a kind of inner speech of the soul, people of old conversed as it were with each planet just as today we converse with one another in ordinary speech. They realized that the movements of the stars in the universe were experienced and reflected in their inmost soul. This was a living, spirit-inwoven conception of the universe ...

On the other hand, an inner experience of the secrets of humanity could arise in specially endowed people such as the shepherds. Once their inner forces reached a certain stage of development, their instinctive, imaginative perception became direct vision. Through this faculty of inner vision the simple shepherds in the fields heard the proclamation of God revealed in the heavenly heights, through whom peace can flow to all people of good will ...

While we live on the earth and unfold the forces which bring knowledge of the world around us, while we unfold the impulses for our actions and social interactions, we unconsciously experience something else as well. We have no knowledge of it but, just as we experience the after-effects of life before birth, so we also experience what finally passes through the gate of death to become the content of life after death. These forces are already present in germ between birth and death but come to full bloom only in the life after death. They were intensely active in the old, instinctive clairvoyance, and in their last echoes they were still working in the simple shepherds, because of their purity of heart. We live within the play of these forces above all during sleep, when the soul moves beyond the body into the outer universe. This is the same form of existence in which the soul will live consciously after death when the physical body has been laid aside ...

The forces active in the human being between death and a new birth can also be kindled during earthly life. This was the case with the three Magi. When it occurs one can experience what is happening beyond the earth, in the cosmos. The human being is transported from the earth into the world of the stars in which he lives between death and a new birth. This was the world into which the three Magi were transported—away from the earth into the heavens ...

The revelation to the shepherds in the fields was the revelation given by the earth, proceeding from their physical nature. In a state of dream the voice of the angel made known to them what had come to pass. And it is entirely in keeping with the Mystery of Golgotha that its revelation came from two sides: to the Magi through heavenly lore, and to the shepherds through the earth ... it is the same proclamation from two different sides.

At the time of the Mystery of Golgotha the soul mood of the shepherds and the Magi was present in its last vestiges, and was transformed in the course of humanity's evolution. What has the wisdom possessed by the Magi now become? It has become our mathematical astronomy. The Magi possessed super-earthly knowledge, which was actually a glorious remembrance of life before birth. This knowledge has shrivelled away into our present conceptions of the heavens, to whose phenomena we apply only mathematical and mechanistic laws. Our modern mathematical astronomy is the meta-morphosis of knowledge once possessed by the Magi.

Our outward, sense-based knowledge, in contrast, conveyed merely through the eyes and ears, is the externalized form of the inner knowledge once possessed by the shepherds in the fields. The mood of soul in which the secrets of earth existence were once revealed to the shepherds now allows us to look at the world with the cold detachment of scientific observation. This kind of observation is the child of the shepherd wisdom — but the child is very unlike the parent! And our mathematical astronomy is the child of Magi wisdom ... The outer has become inward, the inner outward ...

The true reality of the event of Golgotha can no longer be grasped by the forces of knowledge, feeling and belief which we nowadays possess. This event must be discovered anew. The Magi wisdom has become inward, has turned into the abstract mathematical science which is brought to bear in studying the heavens. What has become inward in this way must again be filled with life, re-cast, reshaped from within ...

The Magi comprehended the starry worlds, perceiving in them the spiritual, for they could view human experiences in the life before birth. This has become abstract in our mathematics. But the same forces that our mathematical thinking develops can again be filled with life, can be enriched and intensified in imaginative perception ... We can then behold the outer heavens through inner perception, inner vision, as the Magi once discerned the Mystery of Golgotha through outer perception. The outer has gone inward into mathematical abstraction. Therefore what is now inward must be expanded into perception of the outer universe; inward perception must lead to a new astronomy, to one inwardly, imaginatively experienced.

Only by striving for a new understanding of Christ can we truly celebrate the Christmas festival today. Can we say that this festival still has any real meaning for the majority of people? It has become a beautiful custom to take the Christmas tree as a symbol of the festival. This custom, though, is barely a century old ... when we trace its history it dawns on us that the Christmas tree is directly connected with the tree of paradise. The mind turns to the tree of paradise, to Adam and Eve. This is one aspect of the way the Mystery of Golgotha can be proclaimed again in our time. The mind turns from the Mystery of Golgotha back to the world's beginning. The meaning of world redemption is not understood and the mind turns back to the divine creation of the world. This comes to expression in the fact that the real symbol of Christmas — the crib — so beautifully presented in the Christmas plays of earlier centuries, is gradually superseded by the Christmas tree which is, in reality, the tree of paradise. The old religion of Jehovah gave way to

Christianity, but the Christmas tree is the symbol of its reappearance. This Jehovah religion, however, has reappeared in a multiple and divided way. Jehovah was worshipped—and rightly so—as the one undivided Godhead in an age when his people felt themselves to be a single, self-contained unity not looking beyond their own boundaries, yet full of the expectation that one day they would fill the whole earth. But in our time, although people *speak* of Jesus Christ, in reality they worship Jehovah. In the various nations (this was all too evident in the war) people spoke of Christ but were really venerating the original Godhead who holds sway in heredity and in the world of nature—Jehovah ... The assertion of the principle of nationality, the claiming of national gods, denotes a step backwards into the old Jehovah religion. Those who see fit to worship Christ as a national God are the ones who deny him most deeply.

Let us remember that the proclamations to the shepherds and the Kings contained a message for all mankind—for the earth is common to all. The revelation to the shepherds was from the earth, and as such may not be differentiated according to nationality. The Magi received the proclamation from the sun and the heavens, which was also a revelation destined for all mankind, for when the sun has shone upon one land it moves on to shine on another. The heavens are common to all; the earth is common to all. What is common to all humanity awakens through Christianity. Such is the aspect of Christmas revealed by the twofold proclamation ...

When we think of the Christmas mystery our minds must turn to a birth, to something that must be born anew in our time. True Christianity must be born anew. We need a Christmas festival of the whole cosmos; and it is the intention of spiritual science to prepare the proper ground for such a festival among human beings.

18. From Birth to Rebirth

Extract from a lecture given in Basel on
23 December 1917

*Much like the Magi in T.S. Eliot's 'Journey of the
Magi',[27] Steiner sees the Kings' gifts to the child as token
of their recognition that their form of knowledge is
drawing to an end and must henceforth be sought within
earthly realities instead. He goes on to give one example of
how cosmic wisdom can be discovered as earthly law. In
doing so he explicitly links Christmas with Easter,
showing how the one is fulfilled in the other, and returns
to the vital importance of love for the true perception and
understanding of another. While the tug towards Easter
is absolutely explicit in this lecture, all the lectures in this
volume show Christmas as embedded in the year's over-
arching rhythm, as one of the 'stations' of human
experience and evolution that are all interconnected.
Thus Steiner continually gives us a fluid, dynamic,
mutually interpenetrating sense both of the year's festivals and of their human significance.*

The Magi who brought the symbolic gifts of gold,
frankincense and myrrh to the baby in the manger

were astrologers in the ancient sense. They had knowledge of the spiritual processes that work in the cosmos when certain signs appear in the starry heavens. One such sign they recognized when, in the night between 24 and 25 December, in the year we now regard as that of the birth of Jesus, the sun, the cosmic symbol of redemption and new life, shone towards earth from the constellation of Virgo. They said: 'When the constellation of the heavens is such that the sun stands in Virgo in the night between 24 and 25 December, then an important change will take place in the earth. Then the time will have come for us to bring gold, the symbol of our knowledge of divine guidance, which hitherto we have sought only in the stars, to that impulse which will now become part of the earthly evolution of humanity. Then the time will also have come to offer frankincense, the emblem of sacrifice, the symbol of the highest human virtue. This virtue must be offered in such a way that it unites with the power proceeding from the Christ who is to be incarnated in the human being to whom we bring frankincense. And the third gift, myrrh, is the symbol of the eternal in the human being, which we have felt for thousands of years to be connected with the powers that speak to us from starry constellations. We bring it as a gift to him who is to be a new impulse for humanity, and thus also seek our own immortality, uniting our own souls with the power of Christ. When the cosmic symbol of world power, the sun, shines in the constellation of Virgo, then a new time begins for the earth.' ...

In bringing the divine gifts of wisdom, virtue and immortality to the manger ... the Magi wished to show that from then on the powers that had previously radiated their forces down to earth from the cosmos were no longer accessible in the same way to human beings—that is by gazing into the skies, by study of the starry constellations. They wished to show that the human being must now begin to give attention to the events of historical evolution, to social evolution, to the manners and customs of humanity itself. They wished to show that Christ had descended from heavenly regions where the sun shines in the constellation of Virgo, a region from which all the varied powers of the starry constellations proceed that enable the microcosm to appear as a reflection of the macrocosm. They wished to show that this spirit now enters directly into earthly evolution, which from then on can only be understood by inner wisdom, in the same way as the starry constellations were formerly understood ...

Before the Mystery of Golgotha, in which I include the mystery of Christmas, the Magi studied the heavens when they wished to investigate the secrets of human evolution or any other mysterious event. They studied the constellations, and the relative positions of the heavenly bodies revealed to them the nature of events taking place upon earth. But at that moment in which they became aware of the important event that was happening on earth, by the sign given to them through the position of the sun in Virgo on 24 and 25 December, they said: 'From this time onwards the heavenly constellations themselves will be directly revealed in human affairs on earth.'

Can the starry constellations be perceived in human affairs? ... The period between Christmas and Easter can be seen as corresponding to 33 years ... What does this mean? That the Christmas festival celebrated this year belongs to the Easter festival that follows 33 years later; and likewise that this year's Easter festival has an inner connection with the Christmas of 1884 ... According to our reckoning this period of 33 years is that of a human generation. Thus a complete human generation elapses between Christmas festivals and the Easter festivals connected with them ...

Thus the birthdays or beginnings of events happening today can be found in the events of 33 years before; and today's events are the birthday or beginning of events that will ripen to fruition over the next 33 years ... All the actions of former generations, all the impulses and the deeds connected with them, pour into historical evolution and have a life cycle of 33 years. Then comes the Easter time of these deeds and impulses, the time of resurrection ... All things in historical evolution are transfigured after 33 years, arise as from the grave, by virtue of a power connected with the holiest of all redemptions, the Mystery of Golgotha ...

Just as we calculate the cyclic rotations of celestial bodies so we must learn to calculate historic events by means of a true science of history ...

When we meditate on the mystery of Christmas we do so most effectively if we acquire a knowledge of the secrets of life that need to be revealed in this age in order to enrich the stream of Christian tradition concerning the Mystery of Golgotha and the inner meaning of the Christmas mystery. Christ spoke to humanity in these words: 'Lo! I am with you always even to the end of the world.' ...

No physical scientist can give answers to the questions of the virgin birth and the resurrection. On the contrary, every scientist must inevitably deny these events. They can only be understood when viewed from a plane of existence in which neither birth nor death plays the important part they do in the physical world. Just as Christ Jesus passed through death in such a way as to make

death an illusion and resurrection the reality—
which is the content of the Easter mystery—so did
Christ Jesus pass through birth in such a way as to
render birth an illusion, and 'essential transforma-
tion' within the spiritual world a reality; for in the
world of spirit there is neither birth nor death, only
changes of condition, metamorphoses. Not until
humanity is prepared to look into that world in
which birth and death both lose their physical
meaning will the Christmas and Easter festivals
regain their true significance and sacredness.

Then and only then will our hearts and souls be
filled with the inner warmth which will pervade
what we say to our children, even in earliest
childhood, about the child who was laid in the
manger, and the Three Wise Men who brought to
him their gifts of wisdom, virtue and immortality.
We must be able to speak of these things to children, for what we say to the child about the
Christmas mystery will later be celebrated by him
as an Easter festival, will resurface in his life at the
age of 33. For in historical evolution the responsi-
bilities of humanity are such that one generation
can only express as Christmas impulse those forces
that the next generation will experience as an Easter
impulse. If we could really be fully aware of this,
my dear friends, one generation would think of the
next like this: in the Christmas star I teach you to

receive into your soul as truth what will arise in you as Easter star after 33 years. If we were conscious of this connection between one generation and the next, each of us could say: 'I have received an impetus that extends far beyond today, for the period between Christmas and Easter does not merely comprise the weeks that lie between these festivals but is really a period of 33 years. This is the true life cycle of an impulse that I plant in the soul of a child as Christmas impulse, and which will arise again as Easter impulse after a period of 33 years.

Such things should not foster pride in mere theoretical knowledge. They are of value only when expressed in practical deeds, when our souls become so filled with conviction in relation to them that we are impelled to act in accordance with their light. Only then is the soul filled with love for the great being for whom the deeds are done in this light. Then this love becomes a tangible, specific thing, filled with cosmic warmth, and quite distinct from that sentimental affectation that we find today on all lips but that has led in these catastrophic times to some of the greatest impulses of hatred among humanity. Those who have talked so long about love have no further right to speak of it when it has turned to hatred. Such people should ask themselves instead: 'What have we omitted in our talk of love, of Christmas love, to have enabled hatred to develop from it?' Humanity however must also ask: 'What must we seek in the world of spirit in order to find what has been lost, that love that rules, inhabits and warms all beings, but is only real love when it wells up from a vital understanding of life?'

To love another is to understand him. Love does not mean filling one's heart with egotistical warmth that overflows in sentimental speeches. Love means to comprehend the being for whom we should do something, to understand not merely with the intellect but through our innermost being—to understand with the full nature and essence of our human nature.

That such a love, springing from deepest spiritual understanding, may be able to find its place in human life, that desire and will should exist to cherish such love, may still be possible in these difficult times for anyone willing to tread again the path of the Magi to the manger. Such a person can say to himself: 'Just as the Wise Men from the East sought understanding to find the way, the path of love to the manger, so I will seek the way that will open my eyes to the light in which the true deeds of human love are performed. Just as the Magi surrendered their faith in the authority of the starry heavens, adding to their knowledge of the stars their sacrifice of this knowledge, and bringing to the

Christ child on Christmas night the union of immortality and stellar wisdom, so humanity, in these later times, must offer up its deepest soul impulses as sacrifice to the being annually symbolized in the Christmas festival. Inspired by such a consciousness, the Christmas festival will again be celebrated by humanity sincerely and truly. Its celebration will then express not a denial but a knowledge of the being for whom we light the Christmas candles.

19. Christ Born Within Us

Extract from a lecture given in Berlin on
27 December 1914

*In this passage Steiner touches on his insight that
Christ unites and is embodied in two different aspects:
that of primal, pre-lapsarian innocence as reflected in
the Luke Gospel, and of the highest human wisdom in
the John and Matthew Gospels. These two aspects, in
turn, are closely related to the forms of knowledge
embodied in 'shepherd' and 'Magi' wisdom (see the
introduction to section 17). But the most powerful message of this excerpt is that we need to seek Christ as the
very core of our individual identity — give birth to him
within ourselves — if we are to reconnect meaningfully
with an upward evolutionary path. In other words
Christ is the ultimate fulfilment of human potential, the
archetypal and yet simultaneously actual being who
approaches us from the future, and comes into ever
clearer focus in our inward vision as we approach and
unite with him. In attempting — very slowly through
long ages of evolution — to do so, we need to take full
possession of every dimension of the self, to become, in
other words, completely, consciously individual, and yet*

at the same time grow towards complete accord and
harmony with the cosmos.

> 'Were Christ born a thousand times in Bethlehem
> and not in thee, thou art lost eternally.'

There are two aspects of this beautiful saying by the
great mystic Angelus Silesius. One consists in a
recognition that Christmas can only be truly celebrated in our inmost hearts and that all outward
Christmas celebration should spur us on to grasp
the inner reality which draws the very deepest
powers of the soul up from the depths of darkness
during the Holy Nights—a darkness prevailing in
the soul just as, outwardly, winter prevails. These
deep forces of the soul are aware of their union with
the being who pervades all earthly evolution, and
gives it meaning and purpose. If we descend far
enough into the deep regions of our soul life, where
our consciousness is still open to the spiritual
powers of the world, we find there something
connected with Christ.

The other aspect of the words of Angelus Silesius
is that we, who feel ourselves so human at our
present stage of evolution, can grow conscious of
the fact that our true, essential humanity depends
on the soul feeling inwardly united with the abso-
lute reality of Christ Jesus.

Over the years our studies have brought home to us the fact that as earthly evolution proceeds our awareness of Christ must continually deepen; that human beings passing from incarnation to incarnation must attain ever greater understanding of the real nature of Christ. We have tried to intensify this knowledge by drawing on a source that enables us to celebrate the holy night of Christmas, the festival of Jesus' birth, in a deeper, more worthy way. What this implies will become clear from today's lecture . . .

It is possible for a really learned scholar today to survey the whole course of history without perceiving the Christ power at work everywhere since the Mystery of Golgotha. There are many causes to account for the fact that the festival of the holy night, of the Christmas mystery, is not yet celebrated in the souls of a very large number of human beings . . .

Every human being on the earth is related *individually* to Christ. Folk or national history is interwoven with the affairs and circumstances of all the different cultures and races, for it is concerned with human affairs in general, and with general human destiny. But what Christ Jesus brought into the world penetrates deeply and inwardly into the experiences of every human heart and soul — no matter where it stands in terms of culture or development—in so far as it feels itself truly human. We should realize that this 'feeling human' first arose through the Mystery of Golgotha ...

With all humility, with a humility deeper than that with which we approach any other area of spiritual science, it may truly be said that the best human souls have, for long ages, been yearning and pining for the knowledge of Christ that esoteric science can give. And the time will soon be ripe for human souls to behold, as reality, what they previously knew only through indirect means.

Humanity has very largely lost awareness of the Christ as a cosmic being. This loss was inevitable, for the old clairvoyance had to give way to an intervening period—an age or aeon devoid of spirit—so that eventually a new form of clairvoyant vision may develop. But this new vision must again be directed to worlds of spirit, must not characterize in mere outward forms the being who enters the evolution of humanity in the holy night. This new vision must reveal the Christ being descending through heavenly spheres to the earth, endowing it with meaning and purpose ...

What, in reality, is the earth that surrounds us if we perceive the essence of its nature? If the corpse of someone lies before you, and his soul already dwells in worlds of spirit, can you still say that this is a human being in the full sense of the word? The higher members of human nature no longer dwell in the corpse from which the soul has departed. But since the middle of the Atlantean epoch[28] this is what the earth has gradually become: a corpse devoid of soul. Despite its manifold beauties, the earth around us has been approaching the state of a corpse since the middle of Atlantean times, and is becoming increasingly corpselike. When you stand before huge rocks and cliffs you can see that they are the skeleton which the earth has been in the process of becoming ever since that time. In the rock-strewn earth we perceive the dying part of the earth organism, which was truly alive only until the middle of Atlantean times ... And so, inasmuch as we are surrounded by the earth, we confront death and are spectators of the gradual death of our globe.

But now imagine that the Mystery of Golgotha had not taken place, that the cosmic being whom we call Christ had not entered Earth evolution ... Our evolution on earth would advance no further, would by now already have been overwhelmed by death ... But Christ *did* enter earthly evolution and ... consummated the Mystery of Golgotha. Because of this, when the time is fulfilled, the earth will not remain a corpse nor the soul fall prey to Ahriman and Lucifer,[29] for the Christ seed has infused new life into Earth evolution! Just as

the earth once separated from the sun and became
the sun's offspring, so it will be imbued with the
new meaning and purpose which Christ imparted
to evolution ...

In our time it is again beginning to be possible
for those in whom the impulses of spiritual
science have come to life to look up to the Christ
as a cosmic being. Let us remember, though, that
this does not diminish the infinite devotion we
can feel towards the child born in the holy night
of Christmas. We can feel the reality of Christ
with deep devotion, as did our dear friend Christian Morgenstern, when there sprang from his
soul a poem which seems like a resurrection of
ancient and holy Gnostic thoughts, pervaded
equally by the love of Christ and cosmic wisdom.
We may celebrate a new Christmas when, in the
dark night of materialism, voices resound that are
not those of the past, of ancient Gnostics, but are
quickened and enriched by their dedication to the
living essence of the cosmic Christ.

Light is love ... sun weaving's
love radiance, a creating
universe of beings

who hold us to their heart
through untold ages;
who did at length impart

to us their most sublime
Spirit Lord to live
three years in human form—

and now this selfsame One
is earth's inmost heaven fire,
and earth may now aspire
to be, one day, a sun.[30]

Were Christ born a thousand times in Bethlehem, and not in thee, thou art lost eternally.

May there be celebrated in our souls an inner festival of the holy night; may our souls be filled with the realization that a new knowledge of Christ must be born in our time. This new knowledge of Christ links the inmost core of our being with primal innocence, links the state of childhood with the very heights of cosmic being. When our mind turns to the Christ child in the holy night of winter, the greatest of all festivals of consecration is enacted before our souls, one that resounds through all the ages, and we know that the deepest realities of our nature and being are indissolubly connected with all cosmic evolution.

Those whose hearts are kindled by spiritual science feel that victory over death can be achieved when the soul is united with the Christ being. I spoke of this today at the funeral of one taken from us so tragically by the war. Realization of how the heights of cosmic reality are connected with the inmost nature of the human being was impossible as long as the human mind was unable to perceive the very quintessence of history in the mystery of Bethlehem. But this insight will dawn in those who understand the secret of the two Jesus boys.[31] In the one boy existed the power of Zarathustra, the wisest of all pre-Christian human beings. This boy represents the flower and summation of all previous stages of human evolution. The aura of the other boy was illumined by the forces of the great Buddha. The body of the one boy springs from the noblest blood of the ancient Hebrew peoples, while the soul of the Jesus boy described in the Gospel of St Luke leads back to the earth's beginnings. When the human being embarked on Earth evolution in the age of Lemuria,[32] the soul of the Jesus boy of St Luke was kept back and guarded by the mysteries, and was then sent into the body of the Jesus child whose birth is described in that Gospel ...

Spiritual science enables us to understand the Christ impulse from its source in the deep currents of human evolution, from the evolution of pre-Christian times. When we plumb these depths the differences between our time and the distant past disappear and the initiates speak once more. When the magnitude of what poured into humanity's evolution at the Mystery of Golgotha is grasped it

will become a source of strength to further everything connected with this evolution, including our
understanding of history. But we must know who
the Christ truly was before we can speak of him in a
historical context. If individuals exist in our movement who, in ever greater numbers, resolve to
kindle the light that *can* be kindled in the depths
since the Mystery of Golgotha, then the Christ light
will shine out in every single soul. This Christ light
becomes the Christmas tree that will illumine all
evolution in ages to come. The soul will behold a
rejuvenated earth, within which Christ is omni-
present.

Those who have forged a connection with the
science of the spirit can receive its tidings of Christ
with such depth of feeling that the Christmas festival will one day be celebrated in every individual
soul. It is the festival that represents the birth of that
knowledge of Christ which comes from Christ
himself and is therefore a birth of Christ within us.
True indeed are the words *Were Christ born a thousand times in Bethlehem and not in thee, thou art lost
eternally.* But we can add to this, saying: 'Let us
therefore continually find our own true nature by
seeking repeatedly for the experience of the holy
night of winter, for the birth of Christ in the depths
of our souls.'

20. The Calyx of Mary, the Blossom of Jesus, the Seed of Christ

Extract from a lecture given in Berlin on
22 December 1908

Drawing on the vision of the great poet Novalis, Steiner conjures his own vision of Christ as the potent seed of the future, ripening from humanity's fairest blossom Jesus, and from Mary, this blossom's purest vessel. This powerful and beautiful image recalls old Christmas carols such as 'Es ist ein Ros' entsprungen' ('There is a flower springing'). Like the 'sun at midnight' (see section 8), the blossom born in the very midst of winter, when all other flowers have withered, contradicts the normal course of natural cycles, but for this very reason leads us directly to the non-physical reality which alone gives Christmas its meaning. At the same time, however, this meaning does not deny earthly reality and the physical world but inevitably passes through, renews, and is embodied in it. The spiritual flower cannot blossom without the physical world to root it.

In the case of Novalis we cannot really speak of a single life, for his was like a remembrance of an earlier life. The initiation conferred on him through grace, as it were, brought to life within him his achievements in earlier incarnations; there was a kind of consolidation of insights that had been his in a previous life. And because he looked back through the ages with his own awakened eyes of spirit, he was able to affirm that nothing in his life was comparable in importance to the experience of discovering in himself the real nature of Christ. Such an experience is like a repetition of the event at Damascus when Paul, who had previously persecuted the followers of Christ Jesus, received direct proof through higher vision that Christ lives, is present, and that something took place at the Mystery of Golgotha that is unique in human evolution. Those whose eyes of spirit are open can see this event repeated. Christ was present not only in the body that was once his dwelling place, but has remained united with the earth. Through him the sun power united with the earth.

Novalis speaks of the revelation that came to him as 'unique', and he maintains that only those willing to participate in this event with their whole soul are truly human ... Novalis says that the Christ whom he has seen spiritually is a power permeating all beings ... The eye that beholds the Christ has itself been formed by the Christ power. The Christ power within the eye, he says, beholds the Christ power outside the eye.

These really are powerful words! Novalis is also aware of the mighty truth that since the event of Golgotha the being we call Christ has been the planetary spirit of the earth, the earth spirit by whom the earth's body will gradually be transformed. A wonderful vista of the future opens out before Novalis. He sees the earth transformed; he sees the present earth, which still contains the residue of ancient times, transformed into the body of Christ; he sees the earth's waters permeated with Christ's blood and he sees the solid rocks as Christ's flesh. He sees the body of the earth gradually becoming the body of Christ, the earth and Christ miraculously made one. He sees the earth in future times as a great organism in which man is embedded, and whose soul is Christ.

In this sense, and out of his deep experience of knowledge gained through the spirit, Novalis speaks of Christ as the 'Son of Man'. In a certain sense human beings are the 'sons of the gods', that is to say, of the ancient gods who through untold millions of years have moulded or shaped our planet, who have built our bodies and formed the ground upon which we move. In the same way it is now our human task, by overcoming earthly things through our own powers, to build an earth that will

be the body of the new God, the God of the future.
And whereas human beings of ancient times looked
back to the primeval gods, yearning to be reunited
with them in death, Novalis recognizes the God
who in time to come will have as his body all that is
best in us, that we can offer to form the body of
Christ ...

All these experiences and perceptions are so
deeply significant that they are well able to kindle
the true mood of Christmas in our souls ...

Since the event of Golgotha the spiritual world
has been illumined with an ever brighter light.
Everything existing in the physical world originally
issued from the world of spirit. In olden times when
souls passed from the physical into the spiritual
world, they could say: 'Here is the wellspring and
origin of everything the physical world contains.
The physical world originating from the world of
spirit is only an effect, a reflection of the spiritual
world.' But since the event of Golgotha, when we
pass from the physical into the spiritual world we
can see that there is now also causality in the physical world, and that what is experienced through
the event of Golgotha on the physical plane works
back into the world of spirit.

And so it will continue in ever-increasing
measure. Everything proceeding from the work of
the ancient gods will die away, and what will

blossom forth will live on into the future as the workings of the evolving God. This is what will pass over into the world of spirit. It is just as though someone looking at the seed of a new plant were to say to himself: 'True, it emerged from an old plant, but now the old leaves and blossoms have fallen away and vanished, and now the new seed is there, the seed that will unfold into the new plant and blossom.' We too live in a world where leaves and blossoms fall away and yield divine seeds. Increasingly the new fruit, the Christ fruit, is unfolding, and everything else will fall away. What is striven for and mastered here in the physical world will have value in the future only in so far as it is carried over into the world of spirit. Before our eyes of spirit a world arises in the future, one that has its roots in the physical as our world once originated from the spiritual world. Just as human beings are the sons of gods, so, out of what human beings experience in the physical world by opening to the event of Golgotha, the body will be formed for those new gods of the future, of whom Christ is the leader. So do ancient worlds live on into new worlds; the old dies utterly away and the new sprouts and springs into bud from the old. But this could only come about because humanity was mature enough to unfold a blossom for that spiritual being who was to become the God of the future.

This blossom that could receive into it the seed of the God of the future could only be a threefold human vessel consisting of physical body, etheric body and astral body[33] — a vessel cleaned and purified by all that human beings on earth could attain. This blossom of humanity, this vessel of Jesus of Nazareth, who sacrificed himself so that the Christ seed might be received, represents the very purest essence that the spiritual endeavours of evolving humanity could produce. Not until the earth was ready to bring forth her fairest blossom could the seed for the new God appear. And the birth of this blossom is commemorated in our Christmas festival. At Christmas we celebrate the birth of the blossom that was to receive the Christ seed.

Christmas is actually a festival, therefore, when human beings can gaze both into the past and into the future. From the past has issued the blossom out of which unfolds the seed for the future. The threefold vessel of Christ was a product of the ancient earth — woven and born from the highest the human being could achieve. No outward celebration can make a more powerful impression on us than the insight that the fairest flower of humanity blossomed from the purest calyx ... We see how what is born from the clouds, that is from the spiritual, has densified into the calyx which flowers into the future evolution of humanity. This conception, already known to the ancients, can be rediscovered in the Christian Madonna with the child Jesus.

With supreme purity and delicacy Raphael has breathed this mystery into form in his portrayal of the *Sistine Madonna.* The Madonna condenses out of angels' heads and in turn brings forth Jesus of Nazareth, the blossom which will later receive the Christ seed. The whole story of humanity's evolution is contained in this picture of the Madonna. No wonder then that as he stood before the image of the Madonna there arose in Novalis the most beautiful, glorious remembrance of an earlier incarnation whose memory was, in turn, captured there, and that there germinated in him all the beautiful feelings, the sublime insight that the mystery of humanity depicted in this painting could awaken. No wonder that these feelings streamed to the being from whom Christ was born, to the figure who brought forth the calyx from which sprang the blossom that could allow the seed of the new God to ripen.

And so we see how in the supremely gifted Novalis feelings free of all denominational bias quicken to life at the portrayal of this holy mystery — which was enacted at the first Christmas and is repeated every Christmastide. This is the mystery of the ancient initiates bringing their offerings to the new mystery — the Wise Men who are bearers of the wisdom of times past, who make their offerings to what will continue into the future, which, in a human being, will one day harbour the power pervading all the worlds connected with our earth.

Novalis experienced the Christ mystery, the Mary mystery, in relation to the cosmic mystery. It illumined his soul, just as it had shone at the first Christmas when beings who had never descended to the physical plane proclaimed the union between a cosmic and an earthly power, which can become a reality in human hearts and in the cosmos itself when the human heart unites with Christ. What was true for the Egyptians is now no longer true. They said that the God with whom they must be united dwells in the world that can only be reached after death. Now the God with whom human beings must be united lives among us here, between birth and death; and human beings can find him when they unite their hearts and souls with him in this world ...

At the crux of time
the spirit light of worlds entered
earthly being's onward flow;
darkness of night
had held dominion;
bright light of day
streamed into human souls:
light bringing warmth
to simple shepherd hearts;
light that illumines
kings' wise heads—
God-filled light,
Christ sun,
O warm
our hearts,
illumine
our heads;
so that good may grow
from everything that we
start from our hearts.
From everything that we
try through our heads
to guide purposefully.

Afterword

The lecture extracts in this volume, even when they do not refer to this explicitly, repeatedly circle round the theme of innocence and experience. Humanity's long journey from Eden passes through the needle's eye of the separate ego to an ultimate, and conscious, reunion with its highest self. In the dusty midst of this journey it is easy to dismiss the childhood of humanity, its lost innocence, as a state of ignorance and unknowing, and its future unfolding of the fullest human potential as pie in the sky.

Poets often retain a strong connection with the vibrancy of childhood perception, none more so than Thomas Traherne. The extract from a prose poem quoted below,[34] written in 1671, three years before his death, vividly conjures a state of primal innocence, of pure, unsullied wonder. It seems fitting to end this volume with a reminder of the full, innocent presence of mind that seems so apt a vision of the state of paradise — not just as a place of departure long-since lost, but as a distant destination awaiting rediscovery.

All appeared new, and strange at first, inexpressibly rare and delightful and beautiful. I was a little stranger, which at my entrance into the world was saluted and surrounded with innumerable joys [...]

The corn was orient and immortal wheat, which never should be reaped, nor was ever sown. I thought it had stood from everlasting to everlasting. The dust and stones of the street were as precious as gold. The gates were at first the end of the world, the green trees when I saw them first through one of the gates transported and ravished me; their sweetness and unusual beauty made my heart to leap, and almost mad with ecstasy, they were such strange and wonderful things. The men! O what venerable and reverend creatures did the aged seem! Immortal cherubims! And the young men glittering and sparkling angels and maids strange seraphic pieces of life and beauty! Boys and girls tumbling in the streets, and playing, were moving jewels. I knew not that they were born or should die. But all things abided eternally as they were in their proper places. Eternity was manifest in the light of the day, and something infinite behind everything appeared: which talked with my expectation and moved my desire. The city seemed to stand in Eden, or to be built in Heaven.

The streets were mine, the temple was mine, the people were mine, their clothes and gold and silver was mine, as much their sparkling eyes, fair skins, and ruddy faces. The skies were mine, and so were the sun and moon and stars, and all the world was mine, and I the only spectator and enjoyer of it. I knew no churlish proprieties, nor bounds nor divisions; but all proprieties and divisions were mine: all treasures and the possessors of them. So that with much ado I was corrupted; and made to learn the dirty devices of this world. Which I now unlearn, and become as it were a little child again, that I may enter into the Kingdom of God.

Notes

1. Steiner uses the word 'mystery' not in the modern sense of enigma, but in its older meaning of 'a truth divinely imparted' or a sacrament (*Chambers Dictionary*). In the plural — the mysteries — he also uses it to describe ancient schools of initiation.
2. See the companion volume in this series.
3. See the companion volume in this series.
4. See the companion volume in this series.
5. The ancient Greek designation for 'cosmic soul'.
6. Anthroposophy was the name Steiner gave to his wide-ranging Christ-centred philosophy and practice. Literally it means 'wisdom of the human being'.
7. An advanced future stage of spiritual consciousness.
8. See the companion volume in this series.
9. Lucifer and Ahriman are the two polar forces of evil in Steiner's cosmology. Lucifer tempts us away from the earth while Ahriman fetters us to it. Christ is the balancing mediator between these two. See also the introduction to section 6.
10. See note 9 above.
11. One of the core tenets of Steiner's anthroposophy is that we pass through many lives and thus experience a wide range of different cultures and ages in the

course of our evolution. The lessons from each life are processed by our eternal essence or ego, and form the basis for each new incarnation.

12. The Russian Orthodox Church of course still celebrates Christmas on 6 January.

13. According to Steiner, former planetary states of evolution preceded and prepared our current phase on earth, and he gives these the names of Saturn, Sun and Moon. See *Occult Science, an Outline*, Rudolf Steiner Press, 1969.

14. See note 9 above.

15. For further elaboration of this subject, see also Bernard Nesfield-Cookson, *The Mystery of the Two Jesus Children, and the Descent of the Spirit of the Sun*, and Gilbert Childs, *Secrets of Esoteric Christianity, The Two Martyrs, the Two Families of Jesus, and the Incarnation of Christ*. Both volumes published by Temple Lodge, 2005.

16. A period after death when we adjust to the realities of the spiritual world and learn to exist without a physical body.

17. See section 10.

18. A son of Adam.

19. Steiner is referring here to an actual tree beside which he stands, adorned with roses and a variety of significant symbols. To read this passage in full, with an explanation of all symbols on the Christmas tree, please see the second lecture in *Festivals and Their Meaning*, Rudolf Steiner Press, 2002.

20. This should not be confused with Freud's desig-

nation, nor with the 'selfish', egotistical self. It refers to the highest, most individualized and immortal aspect of our being.

21. See note 16 above.

22. In Steiner's view we possess, apart from our mineralized physical body, an etheric or life body, which we share with the plant kingdom, and an astral or soul body, which we have in common with animals. The etheric body is chiefly associated with rhythms, circulation and habitual ways of doing things, while the astral body is the seat of passions, emotions and soul.

23. A reference to the two Jesus children, see note 15 above.

24. This lecture was given during the Great War.

25. See note 6 above.

26. This lecture was given on 26 December, so the 'cosmic holy night whose approach we await' is, presumably, 6 January, the Epiphany, when Christ descended at the Jordan baptism.

27. This poem, published in *Collected Poems 1909–1935* (Faber and Faber), includes the lines: 'I had seen birth and death, / But had thought they were different; this Birth was / Hard and bitter agony for us, like Death, our death...'

28. A previous stage of humanity, prior to a great deluge which destroyed its culture and civilization. According to Steiner we are now living in the fifth post-Atlantean epoch.

29. See note 9 above.

30. Original German:

> Licht is Liebe ... Sonnen-Weben
> Liebes-Strahlung einer Welt
> Schöpferischer Wesenheiten —
>
> die durch unerhörte Zeiten
> uns an ihrem Herzen hält,
> und die uns zuletzt gegeben
>
> ihren höchsten Geist in eines
> Menschen Hülle während dreier
> Jahre: da Er kam in seines
>
> Vaters Erbteil — nun der Erde
> Innerlichstes Himmelsfeuer:
> Dass auch sie einst Sonne werde.

31. See note 15 above.
32. The first stage of Earth evolution, prior to the Atlantean, during which human beings divided into male and female.
33. See note 22 above.
34. From The Third Century, in *Centuries*, by Thomas Traherne (1637–74).

Sources

(numbers relate to section numbers in this volume)

1. Stuttgart, 25 December 1919, in: *The Incarnation of Ahriman*, Steiner Press, 2006.
2. Berlin, 19 December 1915, in: *The Christmas Thought and the Mystery of the Ego*, Mercury Press, 1986.
3. Dornach, 24 December 1920, in: *The Search for the New Isis, the Divine Sophia*, Mercury Press, 1986.
4. Berlin, 19 December 1915, in: *The Christmas Thought and the Mystery of the Ego*, Mercury Press, 1986.
5. Dornach, 31 March 1923, in: *The Cycle of the Year*, Anthroposophic Press, 1984.
6. Dornach, 7 April 1923, in: *The Cycle of the Year*, Anthroposophic Press, 1984.
7. Berlin, 24 December 1905, in: *The Festivals and Their Meaning*, Rudolf Steiner Press, 2002.
8. Berlin, 17 December 1906, in: *The Festivals and Their Meaning*, Rudolf Steiner Press, 2002.
9. Berlin, 24 December 1912, in: *Festivals of the Seasons*, Anthroposophical Publishing Company, 1928.
10. Hanover, 26 December 1911, in: *The Festivals and Their Meaning*, Rudolf Steiner Press, 2002.
11. *The Dream Song of Olaf Åsteson*, Rudolf Steiner Press, 1989.
12. Berlin, 21 December 1911, in: *Festivals of the Seasons*, Anthroposophical Publishing Company, 1928.

13. Berlin, 17 December 1906, in: *The Festivals and Their Meaning*, Rudolf Steiner Press, 2002.

14. Berlin, 19 December 1915, in: *The Christmas Thought and the Mystery of the Ego*, Mercury Press, 1986.

15. Basel, 26 December 1921, in: *The Festivals and Their Meaning*, Rudolf Steiner Press, 2002.

16. Dornach, 23 December 1920, in: *The Search for the New Isis, the Divine Sophia*, Mercury Press, 1986.

17. Dornach, 23 December 1920, in: *The Search for the New Isis, the Divine Sophia*, Mercury Press, 1986.

18. Basel, 23 December 1917, in: *Et Incarnatus Est*, Mercury Press, 1983.

19. Berlin, 27 December 1914, in: *The Festivals and Their Meaning*, Rudolf Steiner Press, 2002.

20. Berlin, 22 December 1908, in: *The Christmas Mystery: Novalis the Seer*, Mercury Press, 1985.

Further Reading

Rudolf Steiner's fundamental books:

Knowledge of the Higher Worlds
also published as: *How to Know Higher Worlds*

Occult Science
also published as: *An Outline of Esoteric Science*

Theosophy

The Philosophy of Freedom
also published as:
Intuitive Thinking as a Spiritual Path

Some relevant volumes of Rudolf Steiner's lectures:

Easter
Michaelmas
St John's
Whitsun and Ascension

The Four Seasons and the Archangels

For all titles contact Rudolf Steiner Press (UK) or
SteinerBooks (USA):
www.rudolfsteinerpress.com www.steinerbooks.org

Note Regarding Rudolf Steiner's Lectures

The lectures and addresses contained in this volume have been translated from the German, which is based on stenographic and other recorded texts that were in most cases never seen or revised by the lecturer. Hence, due to human errors in hearing and transcription, they may contain mistakes and faulty passages. Every effort has been made to ensure that this is not the case. Some of the lectures were given to audiences more familiar with anthroposophy; these are the so-called 'private' or 'members' lectures. Other lectures, like the written works, were intended for the general public. The difference between these, as Rudolf Steiner indicates in his *Autobiography*, is twofold. On the one hand, the members' lectures take for granted a background in and commitment to anthroposophy; in the public lectures this was not the case. At the same time, the members' lectures address the concerns and dilemmas of the members, while the public work speaks directly out of Steiner's own understanding of universal needs. Nevertheless, as Rudolf Steiner stresses: 'Nothing was ever said that was not solely the result of my direct experience of the growing content of anthroposophy. There was never any question of concessions to the prejudices and preferences of the members. Whoever reads these privately printed lectures can take them to represent anthroposophy in the fullest sense. Thus it was possible without hesitation — when the complaints in this direction became too persistent — to depart from the custom of circulating this material "For members only". But it must be borne in mind that faulty passages do occur in these reports not revised by myself.' Earlier in the same chapter, he states: 'Had I been able to correct them [the private lectures], the restriction *for members only* would have been unnecessary from the beginning.'

The original German editions on which this text is based were published by Rudolf Steiner Verlag, Dornach, Switzerland in the collected edition (*Gesamtausgabe*, 'GA') of Rudolf Steiner's work. All publications are edited by the Rudolf Steiner Nachlassverwaltung (estate), which wholly owns both Rudolf Steiner Verlag and the Rudolf Steiner Archive.

Rudolf Steiner
Easter
An Introductory Reader

Chapters: Can we Celebrate Easter?; The Earth and the
Cosmos; Rising Sun, Nature and Resurrection; Golgotha,
the Central Deed of Evolution; Easter, a Festival for the
Future.

160pp; 978 185584 139 0; £6.99

Rudolf Steiner
Michaelmas
An Introductory Reader

Chapters: Sinking Earth, Rising Spirit; Michael and the
Dragon; Michael, Spirit of Our Age; Towards a Michael
Festival.

160pp; 978 185584 159 8; £6.99

Rudolf Steiner
St John's
An Introductory Reader

Chapters: Midsummer Dream, the Earth Breathes Out;
Finding the Greater Self; 'He Must Increase, I Must
Decrease'; Creating Vision.

112pp; 978 185584 174 1; £5.99

Rudolf Steiner
Whitsun and Ascension
An Introductory Reader

Chapters: Rising to the Clouds, Tethered to Earth;
Suffering's Open Door; All One to Alone to One in All;
Human Freedom and the Word.

128pp; 978 1 85584 169 7; £5.99